Death of an Ordinary Man

Also by Sarah Perry

Fiction
After Me Comes the Flood
The Essex Serpent
Melmoth
Enlightenment

Non-fiction
Essex Girls

Death of an Ordinary Man

SARAH PERRY

JONATHAN CAPE
LONDON

1 3 5 7 9 10 8 6 4 2

Jonathan Cape, an imprint of Vintage, is part of the
Penguin Random House group of companies

Vintage, Penguin Random House UK, One Embassy Gardens,
8 Viaduct Gardens, London SW11 7BW

penguin.co.uk/vintage
global.penguinrandomhouse.com

First published by Jonathan Cape in 2025

Copyright © Sarah Perry 2025

The moral right of the author has been asserted

'*De Corporis Resurrectione*', from John Burnside's collection *Gift Songs*
(Copyright © The Estate of John Burnside) reprinted by permission of A. M. Heath & Co Ltd.

Penguin Random House values and supports copyright. Copyright fuels creativity, encourages diverse voices, promotes freedom of expression and supports a vibrant culture. Thank you for purchasing an authorised edition of this book and for respecting intellectual property laws by not reproducing, scanning or distributing any part of it by any means without permission. You are supporting authors and enabling Penguin Random House to continue to publish books for everyone. No part of this book may be used or reproduced in any manner for the purpose of training artificial intelligence technologies or systems. In accordance with Article 4(3) of the DSM Directive 2019/790, Penguin Random House expressly reserves this work from the text and data mining exception.

Set in 13.5/16pt Garamond MT Std
Typeset by Six Red Marbles UK, Thetford, Norfolk
Printed and bound in Great Britain by Clays Ltd, Elcograf S.p.A.

The authorised representative in the EEA is Penguin Random House Ireland,
Morrison Chambers, 32 Nassau Street, Dublin D02 YH68

A CIP catalogue record for this book is available from the British Library

HB ISBN 9781787336001
TPB ISBN 9781787336018

Penguin Random House is committed to a sustainable future
for our business, our readers and our planet. This book is made
from Forest Stewardship Council® certified paper.

For Rob

*This writing has to do with some things
I saw, felt, & was part of.*

David Jones, *In Parenthesis*

PART ONE
Life

My father-in-law David, who'd soon begin to die, was waiting by the doughnut stand on Yarmouth seafront when he saw a woman dressed something like a fairy entertain a little crowd with tricks. It was the end of summer: the day was fine, the shining tide was going out. The girl at the doughnut stand didn't know what she was doing, or didn't care, and really the fairy's tricks were too distant to make out; but David was a patient man and had no idea time was short, so he was happy to wait and watch. Robert, my husband and his son, was waiting with him. They were men who enjoyed themselves easily, with a determination to see the best of things: serve them a bad meal and they'd only say what a treat it had been, and almost persuade themselves it was true. So they cheered at the fairy when the crowd cheered, and laughed when the crowd laughed. Their hands were in their pockets. They looked alike, they walked with a similar gait: nobody would have taken them for anything but a father and his son.

I'd wandered away from them to stand in a temper on the shore. I was in the dissatisfied and shiftless state that always settles on me when I've finished a novel, and am faced with what I've done and failed to do. This had made me irritated by the fairy and the crowd and even by the men, both of whom I'd loved most of my life; so I stood sulking alone where the sea withdrew from the sand. But when I heard the girl call that our doughnuts were ready, I ran to pay for them, and took them over to the men in a scalding paper bag. We'd had fish and chips for lunch, and the doughnuts were misshapen and small, but all the same David ate four. They gave him pleasure partly because they were delicious and hot, and partly because they put him in mind of holidays in Yarmouth forty years before, when Robert was a happy and solitary boy who played hours of crazy golf and read second-hand books in bed. David's false teeth were broken, and this made it difficult for him to eat tidily, so bits of doughnut were gathering in his clothes with scraps of the fish and chips he'd eaten earlier. He wore tan-coloured trousers that never needed ironing, and a cotton jacket zipped against the sea wind. He had beautiful white hair which had grown thin only late in life, and showed in tufts under a baseball cap that was badly frayed at the peak. His face was round and snub-nosed, and he was prone to eczema; when he smiled, which he did often, he had dimples. He was clumsy with his hands, and because of this the lenses of his glasses were always smeared, and I worried he saw the world through rising mist. Lately he'd taken to wearing beautiful handmade shoes, and these were curious against the polyester hems of his trousers. When he finished the last doughnut he rubbed cinnamon sugar from his fingers and pressed his shoulder briefly against mine with a familiar affectionate nudge: 'Excellent,' he said. 'That was excellent.'

Now the sun was going down: gulls were screaming over the shuttered doughnut stand, and the fairy was collecting money in a plastic cup. 'It's getting on,' I said.

'Yes,' said David, and looked at me with shy expectancy, because we were going to the circus at the Hippodrome, and he'd seen the tickets in my pocket. He knew the circus well from his holidays in Yarmouth over the years, and often he'd said I should see the famous stage that in the interval would sink by several feet and fill with water. 'Yes,' he said, 'off we go,' and laughed. He was always laughing with a kind of private delighted chuckle that was sometimes difficult to account for; but that afternoon I knew it had to do with the shabby stage disappearing underwater, and the circus-girls in their soaking costumes shedding sequins in the pool.

I took his arm. I looked again at the sea. In the dusk the shine was gone from the water, which looked now like a bolt of dull grey cloth. But I'm not sure David noticed, and it didn't occur to me to tell him that he ought to stand there and look, and marvel over the effect of that declining light; that really he ought to remember it for the rest of his life, which is to say for a little less than two months.

When I was young, I worked in a civil service department where I wrote speeches and briefings on policies I barely understood. This department was confined in the basement of what had once been a grand hotel off the Strand. No light came in. Clocks like the clocks in railway stations meted out the hours. The carpets were grey; so were the desks, the chairs, and the soft partitions that divided hundreds of civil servants from each other. I knew then, and had always known, that I wanted nothing but to be a writer, and wanted it with such a desperate sense of purpose I never wrote a single phrase. To preserve myself against that basement office and its deadening grey, I'd print out poems to memorise, and pin them above my desk (my colleagues, I remember, dealt with me quite kindly). One of these was Shakespeare's Sonnet 65, which deplores time's destruction of brass and stone and earth and boundless sea, and mourns that nothing can withstand the 'wrackful siege of batt'ring days' – nothing, that is (or so he thinks), 'unless this miracle have might: That in black ink my love may still shine bright.'

I used to wonder then what love I might eventually preserve against the rot of time, when the day at last came that I was able to write. An ordinary life wasn't for me, or what on earth would I write about? What I needed was something along the lines of a lost child, who'd die in my lap with lashes spiked with tears; or possibly a friend I'd love as much as Tennyson loved his Hallam, and who'd die young and leave me with half my daily light. Sonnet 65 calls life's loveliest things 'time's jewels', and what I wanted was to hoard rubies and lose them, and spill ink into the loss. But now I understand there are no ordinary lives – that every death is the end of a single event in time's history: an event so improbable it represents a miracle, and irreplaceable in every particular. So here I am, counting out the particulars of my father-in-law's life, and trying to preserve them in ink – it's precious that he drank weak Yorkshire tea in footed mugs printed with blue flowers, and artificially sweetened with tablets he called 'depth charges' as he jettisoned them in, laughing at his own joke. It's precious that he disliked dogs, but could calm a feral cat; precious that he kept sugar-free mints in his pocket, and would thumb them free from the tube and into his mouth without looking; precious that each summer he grew rather tough green beans and froze them to be eaten at Christmas, and had a weakness for ice cream, but could never tolerate broccoli; that he loved Mahalia Jackson, *American Graffiti*, the *Antiques Gazette*, the history of the stamps of the Commonwealth, sudoku puzzle books, a pair of deerskin slippers he prized almost too much to wear – all of this remarkable only because it can never be repeated or retrieved.

He'd been born in summer at the end of the Second World War. His father was a teacher, and his mother raised four sons in a rented flat at the top of a London terrace. The flat was small and dank, and overlooked a yard with chickens squabbling under shared lines of washing. His grandfather had been a warehouseman, and all his life David remembered the old man drinking tea from the saucer when it was too hot for the cup, and each year setting fire to the chimney to burn out the soot and save a shilling on the sweep. When David was a boy of ten, thin and spare from a diet on the ration and with shin splints from having grown up too fast, he moved with his family to a modern house in Basildon, and here his parents sunbathed under Essex skies marvellously clear of London smog, and grew vegetables and soft fruit. In those days the little back gardens were divided only by waist-height wire fences, so that it was possible to see other children playing outside other houses down the ranks of lawns, and David's parents would take their chairs into the front garden when the sun was in that direction, and sit drinking tea and speaking to passers-by.

When in 1970 David married Robert's mother Jenny, and had his own Basildon house not far from where his parents still lived, Jenny would sit on sunny days in the front garden and raise her mug of sweet tea to anyone pausing for a chat. Then for some reason this stopped being the custom, and neighbours retreated behind their front doors and raised their garden fences; so that by the time I first visited their home nobody would ever have dreamed of doing such a thing, and it seemed mad to think they ever had.

The Yarmouth Hippodrome is set back from the seafront opposite a violently cheerful amusement arcade. Its art nouveau columns and arches are a little marred by time and sea weather, but this makes them more lovely, not less. Headed there through the slow dusk, I lagged behind the men. They'd been there before, decades ago when Jenny was alive, and because of this I began to feel quite separate from them, as if they were distant from me not by forty yards but forty years. When we went in, I felt that I could see all the years preceding still visible under the present: that white-haired David was also a young father with his young son; that Jenny was dead, but also going laughing in her wheelchair down the narrow, glamorous corridors that smelt of burnt popcorn and fresh paint. We took our seats, and when I sat between Robert and his father, I interrupted time.

It was the last day of the Hippodrome's summer spectacular. The circus was full, and there was a kind of desperate gaiety in the air, as if this would be the measure of all summer: the one thing remembered when the frost set in. The central stage was red, and so were the seats and the carpeted aisles; red and yellow banners were suspended drooping overhead.

'Do you remember it?' I said, and the men said laughing that yes, they remembered it very well — that in fact they hardly needed memory, since nothing much had changed.

'We always sat in the front,' said Robert, 'just there, because of Mum's wheelchair. And sometimes I was frightened because the clowns would come leaping off-stage into somebody's lap, and that would have broken all her bones. But they must have seen her chair, because they never did.'

'They'd pretend to throw buckets of water,' said David, 'and the audience would scream and hide and make a terrible racket. Of course it was just cut-up bits of newspaper in the bucket, but every year we screamed all the same.' Then he was laughing again, not in his shy secretive way but with an expansive joy that took in the stranger on his left. All his life he'd endured the English reserve which despises above everything the possibility of being noticed in a crowd, but this was obliterated by his pleasure in our company, and his willingness to find everything wonderful and ridiculous – the Egyptian juggler bafflingly dressed as Michael Jackson, the Scottish compère who declared over and over 'I'm enjoying myself! I'm enjoying myself!' as he tripped in pools of water. Often when David laughed, his body in the shabby velvet seat shook with the vitality of his good humour, and I'd receive this into my own body until I was laughing, too. In the interval, as the stage began to sink and fill, we bought a bag of candyfloss and picked at it, saying that really we might as well be eating poison; and 'It hasn't changed,' said Robert, 'it really hasn't changed at all.'

But in fact the Yarmouth we walked through that day was laid over a dozen vanished versions of itself, each containing vanished versions of the men who sat either side of me watching the Hippodrome flood. Towards the end of the 1970s, when David was a young industrial chemist at the May & Baker factory, he took his family to stay each year at a Yarmouth hotel which Robert all his life remembered as being immense, imposing, capable of losing children in deep-carpeted corridors. Now it resembles a bail hostel, and behind mottled windows the curtains are coming off their hooks; but once there'd been a grand white façade, and behind it a kidney-shaped pool in a garden with terracotta roof tiles topping the wall. It was owned by a Mr and Mrs Christmas, who were kept permanently tanned by winters spent in Spain. Those were the years when it was common to pay for a room full board, and so the family would dash back from the beach and promenade to the cool, dim dining room for lunch; then in the evenings Mr Christmas would fetch bottles of wine for the rare diners who ordered them, and make a show of removing the cork. David at home was sometimes withdrawn or severe, depleted by commuting on the Fenchurch Street line, and by caring for a child and a disabled wife; but driving to Yarmouth from Basildon – a journey which seemed to Robert a straight line through nothing, joining the only two towns in the world – he'd shed his anxieties county by county, and arrive at the coast an altered man. One summer, struck by mischief, he amused himself by draining the milk jug on the breakfast table each morning, causing the exasperated Mrs Christmas to provide a fuller and fuller jug until on the final day it was spilling over, and David triumphantly drank it by the glass, laughing to himself about it for months – *Heh! Heh! Heh!* All this was before I was born, but became in time so defining a characteristic of him that I've filched the memory of a young man whose black hair grew madly from a double crown, chuckling over his little misdemeanour.

Occasionally in bad weather they'd sit with other families in the TV lounge, or David would play with Robert on the solitary Space Invaders machine – but the weather was always good, or seemed to be. There was the daily walk up and down the length of the promenade, Jenny basking in her wheelchair, which sometimes they manoeuvred on to the sand between deckchairs hired for ten pence from a man who never wore a shirt, and handed out change from a leather pouch tied to his belt. David couldn't swim, and wouldn't try; so Robert as a child was buffeted alone in the North Sea tides while his father dozed in his deckchair over a book of crossword puzzles, or fetched a 99 Flake for himself and the boy, and always a Cornetto for the wife. He didn't particularly feel the heat, and never wore sunscreen; his hair was thicker than a hat. He had then and for most of his life the implacable health of a dray-horse, and in common with all the Perry men the failures of his body were mechanical, not constitutional: teeth that crumbled like chalk, a repeated hernia, hips that wore down and were replaced, and all of this noticed only at the last minute, with embarrassment and irritation at having had to mention it at all. Summer followed summer, and Yarmouth offered pleasure without surprise: it was as far as he ever thought to travel, and each year he set his deckchair three feet from the boundary of the sea and never crossed it.

After the circus ended and brought down the curtain on summer, David went slowly with us up the promenade in the evening chill, favouring a hip aching from confinement in the narrow chair, and going on laughing in his private gleeful way at the flooded stage, the Scottish compère's shrieks, the juggler's white gloves. 'That was splendid,' he said, 'wasn't it excellent!'; then he kissed me, and shook Robert's hand (I saw a kiss between them only once), and drove himself home. During the pandemic he'd moved to the edge of Norwich, where Robert and I have lived for some years. He'd chosen a bungalow in a suburb full of bungalows, where retired men and women live comfortably in small solid homes of red brick, with pitched roofs of terracotta tiles that grow pleasant curds of moss. When David reached home he went slowly up the path beside his artificial lawn, and thought to himself that he'd probably eaten too much, but what a pleasure it would be to sit in his own armchair with its rubbed tapestry seat that faced the television, and watch an episode of *Countdown* or *Antiques Roadshow*, or any of the programmes with which he'd measured out the decades of his life. Some other evening he might have gone to the spare room where his stamp collection was stored, and which had really been a life's work (my earliest memories of David, in the year I fell in love with his son, are of a quiet white-haired man stooped over a table with varnish worn thin by his elbows, and sorting his stamps into packets). But he was tired – that would be the sea air, he thought, and the walk along the promenade – he put the kettle on. There was a calendar beside the kettle, with YARMOUTH CIRCUS written in capitals that signified his excitement. Now that was over – pleased with himself and with us all he marked it with a tick; in the morning he'd cut back the lavender, think about Robert's birthday coming up, remind himself of what else the year contained.

Invariably in the evenings he ate a bowl of cereal before bed, but when he opened one of the packets of porridge he always had in store, he fumbled the seal and scattered oats across the kitchen counter and between his feet. He looked at this mess for a time, and felt he was more tired than he ought to have been, with no inclination to fetch the dustpan and brush. Never curious about himself, he shrugged, poured weak Yorkshire tea into a footed mug with blue flowers printed on it, dropped artificial sweeteners in; turned off the kitchen light, and went through to the chair that increasingly had taken on the imprint of his body. When he sat, he sighed with relief as much as with pleasure, and set the mug down on the coffee table which had held his tea, his magazines and notebooks, since the first days of his marriage, back when nobody would have thought its heavy iron frame and inlaid brown tiles ugly. Then he thought again of the torn paper in the kitchen, and the mess he'd made of the oats. Certainly that was strange, but it was all right, he thought, he'd do it in the morning. He had plenty of time.

PART TWO
Death

John Jarrold, who died at thirty of a raging fever, opened a grocer's and draper's shop in Norwich in 1770. His descendants – mindful of advice he left in a notebook containing recipes for lime pickle, love poems, and instructions never to speak too little or too much – opened a larger shop on London Street. That has now become a handsome department store that sails towards the market square resembling the prow of a ship: in late November every year it's wrapped in red ribbon and presented to the town as a gift. David had a fondness for beautiful things that would have surprised anyone who saw the frayed peak of his baseball cap, and because of this he was fond of Jarrolds, where it's possible to buy a single candle for £370, and be served dots of caviar a few yards from the ladies' toilets. So when he arranged to meet us in town, which he often did, it was always at the Jarrolds prow, where – standing between window displays of this season's shoes and bags – you're sheltered from rain or sun under a curved stone canopy, and can hear the buskers playing a few windows further down. From here the market square takes on the look of a jigsaw puzzle in which you can never hope to match the heads and coats of all the people passing by, and David waiting there would always think what a surprise and a blessing it was that he'd pitched up, quite late in life, in a cathedral city he loved. 'I still feel as if I'm on holiday,' he'd say, 'isn't it funny,' repeating this to waitresses and shop assistants whenever they asked if perhaps he was only visiting for the day.

Not quite three weeks after Yarmouth's summer circus closed, we waited for David in our usual place. He'd seen in the local paper reports of an autumn afternoon tea being served in the Assembly Rooms, and thought it would do for Robert's birthday treat: 'They have biscuits shaped like leaves,' he'd told me over the phone, 'and cakes that look like mushrooms, only those spotty red ones that are poisonous. *Heh! Heh!*' He never forgot birthdays, which each January he entered into a new calendar, and marked with a tick to confirm that a card had been sent (though lately, without knowing why he did it, he'd taken to marking some days with savage cross-hatchings of black pen that almost scored the paper through).

He was late that day. It was overcast, though rain held off; not one of those Keatsian autumn days of illuminated mists, but a dreary vision of the coming winter. 'This isn't like him,' said Robert — it was ten minutes past the hour, and none of us was ever late.

'Probably the buses,' I said, and scanned the shoppers in the market square, but felt no concern, only possibly irritation because I was cold. Then abruptly David was presented to us out of the crowd from a distance of a hundred yards or more, as though the sun had penetrated the low white cloud and sought him out. His sideways-leaning gait had become more pronounced, as if the pavements were bucking and trying to throw him off. Perhaps because of this he had an expression of extreme concentration as he walked, staring not at his feet but fixedly ahead; his skin even at that distance had the thick, dull look of putty. He went on walking with the determination of a man underwater coming slowly up for air; his gaze was directed at us, but without understanding or greeting; he had his baseball cap on.

I've never had the gift of second sight. When I seek out shades and devils in dark corners, I never find them: visions come to me only when sleeping or drugged, and whenever I see angels they revert too soon to pigeons startled in a shaft of sun. My mother taught me maths, my father taught me physics, and the faith of my childhood was the brute logic of Calvinism: I've always been afraid that I'm too governed by reason, and far too sane for prophecies. But watching David come towards me I knew immediately, and with the cool and perfect certainty of arithmetic, that he was more or less a dead man. Oh! I thought, experiencing then no fear or confusion, Oh, he has weeks left, if even that – there was death in his gait, in his grim and concentrated stare, in the dense grey pallor on his cheek. I heard it as clearly as if every person coming behind me through the door with their bags of shopping had whispered it over their shoulder as they passed – *He is a dead man, he is a dead man walking, he is dead.* What could account for this, when really what I saw was only a man in his seventies whose hip sometimes ached, who perhaps had not slept well? I hadn't seen the oats spilled on the kitchen counter, or the calendar with its savage entries of confused black marks; he'd made no complaints of pain, had not coughed or wiped away blood – my understanding arrived out of nothing, could never have been justified, but was accepted without question.

David, making his way, seemed abruptly to recognise us, and this softened the terrible grimness of his expression – but 'he is dead', I thought again, and then my certainty was displaced by sadness that was also in its way a prophecy. I looked at Robert then. We had passed too many years in each other's company for it to be necessary to speak. Difficult to remember whether I took his hand. I hope I did.

'Oh, Robert,' I said. 'My love –'

'Yes,' he said. 'Yes, I see. I know.'

⁓

Once, when I was told this person or that one had died, I'd think of death as a moment of termination, confined to the last moment when the heart stops and the starved brain fails. I imagined that I'd live, then I would die, my death a brief stop at the end of my sentence. Now I understand that death has a duration and an amplitude, with events as various and strange as those of a life. So though it's not possible for me to say when David began to die, I've fixed on that dreary afternoon by the market square, and think of him now in these terms: that he lived for seventy-seven years, and he died for forty-eight days.

⁓

Early in the evening of that same day, we left David at the bus stop in the dark, alone among the shoppers and students heading back to Sprowston or Heartsease or the university campus on the outskirts of town. For three hours we'd kept up a desperate and bewildered good cheer as he disconsolately cut small exquisite sandwiches into smaller and more exquisite pieces, then left them on his plate. 'I just got in a bit of a muddle,' he'd said, apologising for his lateness, and holding on to the tea-room menu without reading it. 'It was all a bit of a muddle.' Then effortlessly, as if pulling a dead weight behind him, he tried to summon the merriment the occasion demanded: 'Doesn't it look excellent,' he said, 'it looks really excellent.'

Still we'd said nothing about that curious lurching walk of his, or the queasy cast of his skin. It would have seemed an impertinence. Under his shyness, and his ability to find silliness everywhere in the world, he had a tough and sometimes irritable spirit, and I knew better than to speak to him about politics for example, since I'd be bested in the fight. Once, I remember, there'd been a story in the news about a man who'd killed his wife as she endured extreme pain from cancer in her breast, and then done a poor job of cutting his own throat, and I'd said that I felt assisted dying was a good thing, and that really the poor widower should never have been hauled before the magistrate with a bandage on his neck. David, driving me home at the time, had shown a sharp sudden flash of his intelligence: 'Absolutely not,' he said, 'never, we should never have that.' His shy benevolent interest in individuals butted up against his cynicism about the nature of mankind as a whole – and really, he seemed to be saying, you couldn't trust pharmacists or doctors as far as you could throw them. Harold Shipman, he said, had been able to get away with it because of some lamentable pharmaceutical accounting practices that he explained, but which I didn't understand. 'We'd see a lot more of that sort of thing,' he'd said darkly, 'you mark my words.' He was no old man to be managed and cajoled: he was the chairman of the board, Robert's chief of staff, the head of our family of three. But towards the end of the meal, as he pressed a piece of scone into a pellet, I said: 'David, do you feel very ill?'

'I just don't feel right.'

'You felt so tired this summer,' I said. 'Do you remember that?'

'Yes,' he said, 'we were all so tired, weren't we?', and this was true: that August a spiteful heatwave had left us all inert indoors, and for days we'd complained over the phone about the impossibility even of taking a walk. 'And things do taste funny,' he said, 'I've gone right off peas. But remember the doctor said that was probably Covid, it's very common. It's just that now things get stuck, and won't go down.'

'I think,' said Robert, 'you should see the doctor again. You do seem to have lost weight.'

'They wanted me to lose weight,' said David, who'd diligently followed a childish NHS handbook on fending off type 2 diabetes, and been commended by the nurse for the loss of a kilogram or two. 'I was supposed to lose weight, they told me to, they were pleased.'

'Even so,' I said. 'Just a check-up.'

Impatient because he was anxious, David said, 'I don't know. All right. Next week. The week after' – he was busy, he said, he had to get to Morrisons, there were things to do. Robert and I looked at each other, and together arrived at a tone that was bolstering and firm without ever conceding that he'd become infirm, or could be told what to do: this week would be a good idea, possibly even tomorrow – 'All right, all right,' said David, not bad-temperedly precisely, but rebuffing us, the doctor, the inconvenience of having a body – 'all right, I'll call tomorrow. Or the day after.' And it was because of this rebuffing – though it seems to me now that it was also because of a failure of our courage – that eventually we left him there at the bus stop, seeming dwindled down to the size of himself as a schoolboy, his pallor sickened by the traffic lights and his knees bony through his trousers: to suggest he couldn't make it home would have been like deposing our head of state, when we could never elect another.

I have a friend who is a writer and a doctor, and because he is a doctor I find it difficult to speak with him about sickness. But walking home through an underpass where boys were setting out their spray cans of paint, I texted him: 'Sam, if someone finds it difficult to swallow, and food tastes funny, should we be worried?' Then quickly and kindly, with an oncologist's authority – and from a man who'd never seen David, and never would – there was this: 'My concern would be oesophageal cancer.'

David, conceding in the end that he wasn't right, really wasn't right at all, was seen that week by a GP whose youth — Robert later told me this — seemed to have made her diligent and cautious. She assessed herself as much as she assessed him, taking his history and his blood pressure as if he represented an exam she couldn't afford to fail. This made David warm towards her, and that cheered him because there was the sense that he wasn't inconveniencing her, or depleting the scarce resources of the NHS, but rather bolstering her confidence and her career. 'It's just that I feel a bit off,' he told her, while Robert listened from a second chair set a little further from her desk. 'Sometimes I get in a muddle, and things get stuck when I eat'; and never, in the days that followed, did he find better ways to explain his depletion, or — when it finally reached him — the pain. Now and then, leading prayer in the Baptist chapel a stone's throw from Norwich railway station, he would speak of redemption and eternity and the availability of grace; but when it came to the matter of his own body he could never find the words, only say again and again that he was in a muddle.

'Fatigue, then,' said the careful young GP, who'd perhaps been taught that the sound of hooves more likely signal a horse than a zebra, 'and there are alterations to your sense of taste. I imagine you've had Covid — perhaps this has been mentioned to you already? — it can present asymptomatically, but still leave you with long Covid, which would account for the tiredness.' That seemed to be the end of it — she'd passed her test, David had passed his – but Robert intervened: 'Don't you think he should have a blood test?'

The GP was doubtful, perhaps because resources of time and needles and laboratories were scarce, or because her comfortable diagnosis had been queried. 'I really think he should,' said Robert, 'please'; and this was difficult for a man who'd never insisted on anything for himself, and shared his father's unwillingness to contradict. Carefully the GP considered this; then – and reluctantly, as if fearful of losing a mark and dropping a grade – she conceded that yes, perhaps after all that mightn't be a bad idea.

David, returning to the waiting room, felt less muddled then. He was a chemist, and trained to see the world as consisting of bonds between molecules: what was he but a series of chemical compounds to be examined and understood, and if necessary amended, possibly even with other compounds made in the laboratory where he'd once worked? But now he needed to approach the reception desk and make another appointment, and he could only do this after a time, and with his old anxious habit of moving forwards almost sideways, apologising with his body for having made it necessary to speak at all.

The woman at the desk was younger even than the GP. Oh, right, needed a blood test did he? Fine. Name? Date of birth? She looked briefly up without seeing him; she looked down. There was a long silence in which she scrutinised the screen in front of her in exasperation, and David thought perhaps he ought to apologise that he was tired, that he could no longer stomach peas.

'Nothing for three weeks, sorry,' she said, offering the date, 'will that be all right?'

'I expect so,' said David, 'yes, I expect that'll be all right,' and thanked her, and prepared to leave; but behind him Robert – with his father's half-apologetic gait – came forward and said, 'But couldn't he go to the walk-in centre, and get it done today?'

'Yeah, if he likes,' said the girl, shrugging. 'Yes, he can do that if he wants. I'd have to print off a form.'

'Well,' said Robert, 'could you do that then, please?', and she did. That evening what we talked about wasn't only David himself, but how bewildering it was that this girl, who'd chosen to work with the sick, hadn't bothered to mention that he needn't wait; and that we couldn't tell, and would never know, whether this was because she'd forgotten, or because she didn't care.

Then, for a week or two, David rallied, or seemed to. We began to doubt our powers of second sight, though never entirely: that vision of death persisted like the hymns we used to know by heart. One evening I cooked him chicken supreme and rice, because my mother had often cooked this when I was young and it made me think of her; and when he ate more than half what he was given I phoned her and said that after all things weren't so bad as they'd seemed. His blood was taken at the clinic without any trouble, and they said he'd hear from them soon; his muddy pallor went, and there were things to be getting on with – what did the council's bin-collection schedule or Norfolk's slow turn towards winter care for the cotton wool that covered the puncture in the crook of his arm? The lawn behind the bungalow should be cut one last time, and what remained of the bean plants needed clearing away, the troughs made ready for spring – and look: already the winter-flowering almond was in bloom, though the geraniums on the patio refused to concede the end of summer and went on in red flower. One Sunday morning he felt too weary for church, and this was unusual – but still he attended to the birthdays on his calendar, though sometimes without thinking he marked the pages with incomprehensible black marks that consumed two or three days at a time.

We visited him every day with Janey and Ruby – our gentle sighthounds, prone to despair, who'd won the affection of a man who'd only ever liked cats – and he kept up his habit of having treats for them ready at the door. He made us weak cups of instant coffee which later in the car I'd complain tasted of dishwater; he identified vulgar and priceless silverware in the *Antiques Gazette* he knew I'd find as funny as he did. I began to doubt myself, and could no longer see death, but when I woke every hour or so in the night I'd remind myself that a thing doesn't disappear because it's out of sight. Often I texted my friend Jude, because her nature was always calmer and more practical than mine, and I relied on her to dampen my fear. 'Sometimes I think I must be going mad,' I said; and much later she told me she'd thought it possible I'd misjudged the situation, and that things weren't as bad as they seemed. And this often occurred to me, too – perhaps I'd taken fright that afternoon outside Jarrolds because David was getting older, and consequently so was I – that at worst he'd developed one of those slower cancers that set up late in life and become a chronic nuisance. Besides, by my nature and profession I can't resist a good story, and *I saw death in the market square* is a better prospect than *my father-in-law is unwell*: who'd put it past me, of all people, to see a storm in a blue-flowered cup of sweetened Yorkshire tea?

But against all my doubts and premonitions, I had one bare fact to set: more and more, and with no logic I could see, David was off his food. We were a family who loved to eat, and plan to eat – all my life I'd been making his favourite dessert of pavlova, delighting in his second helpings and sometimes even in his third; we ate Indian takeaways from trays on our laps, fish and chips on Formica tables, crab sandwiches in a Norfolk café that one winter fell from the cliff on to the beach in a lull between storms – he liked Christmas cake, Müller Fruit Corners, my mother's lemon meringue pie, hot chocolate, scones buried an inch deep beneath yellow clotted cream. His disinclination to eat seemed to be psychological as much as mechanical, and since there were days I saw him swallow cheerfully and without difficulty, and others where he seemed not to have eaten at all, it was difficult to judge whether he was unable to eat, or simply didn't feel like it.

What I didn't understand was that already he was dying – that it was because he was dying, and not only because of the tumour's obstruction, that he was more and more often refusing his food. Sometimes these days

I find I'm angry, because this ought to have been familiar wisdom to me, as familiar as knowing that for example a pregnant woman will frequently be sick. In the aftermath, seeking out stories not of grief but of dying, I saw that to refuse food – placidly, obstinately, and without hunger – is common and unremarkable in the last days of life. It's said of Elizabeth I, for example, that she lay on a pile of cushions, and that 'all about her could not persuade her, either to take any sustenance, or to go to bed . . . there was no hope of her recovery, because she refused all remedies.'

Failing to understand, I became exasperated. I complained to my mother that it was absurd, it was maddening: he could eat a biscuit if he wanted to, I'd seen it, and a man who can eat a biscuit on Tuesday could surely eat toast on Wednesday. He wasn't helping himself, that was the trouble, it was only three weeks since he'd stood eating doughnuts in Yarmouth as the sun went down and told me they were excellent, really excellent. My mother said I should let him be: he wasn't old or feeble enough to need our daily visits, my fretful and managing phone calls – he was only seventy-seven, and in his right mind, and no doctor had suggested he should be forced to eat. Besides, soon enough the blood test would show what the trouble was, and my instincts were all very well, but no substitute for the expert examination of blood cells and platelets and so on. Still: I'd seen death, and if it had moved briefly out of sight I caught it sometimes, out of the corner of my eye – in David choosing jogging bottoms instead of belted trousers for example, and in the thickening smears on the glasses he was neglecting more than ever to clean. One evening I phoned and asked for his weight, and – on the back of a torn and tea-stained NHS envelope, which I have here with me now – I calculated the calories required to keep a man of his size and age alive. Then I stood late into the night preparing soft food I thought he'd like, and which would fuel the idling engine of his body: tomato soup thickened with red lentils and olive oil; mashed potato made nauseatingly rich with a pint of whole milk and all the butter in the house. I bought stacking plastic containers and portioned it out, and Robert took them to David with our love, and our pleading insistence that he eat. But he never did; and months later – when the bungalow was emptied of David's stamp collection, his blue cotton pyjamas, his copies of the *Antiques Gazette* – we found we'd turned the freezer off in the days after his death without emptying it first, and that consequently food had rotted into a peculiar black slime with an unspeakable texture I've never seen in any other substance. I looked for those plastic containers, and couldn't find them; and it was only on this day that Robert told me how, on his visits to the bungalow after his father died, he'd diligently eaten everything I'd made, unable to see an act of love be wasted.

At about this time Robert began to make notes on his phone, which he neither mentioned nor shared until two years after David had died and I began to write this book. In them I see the fear and frustration he never expressed at the time, I suppose because he privileged his father's peace of mind, and mine, above his own, and I'm ashamed not to have noticed how often and how silently he'd been stooped over the phone, making a record of things:

> ... he is literally giving up. He's wondering if he's got 'something major'. Looks very sleepy and distracted. Confused. I asked him what he watched on television last night and he said I had some milk ... asked about what time he got up. Halfway through his replying sentence he started to talk about buses for 5 minutes. I'm not happy about this ...

Sometimes, the notes take on the fractured look of bad verse:

> Tiredness and calories.
> No joy here.
> Bus milk bus milk bus milk bus milk bus milk bus milk.

Then David – preoccupied then, as he'd always been, with buses, birthdays, the increasing difficulty of sudoku puzzle books, and the purchase of milk; the handwriting on his calendar becoming illegible even to himself, and sometimes obscured by scribbled blots – was called and told that his blood test had shown trouble of some kind, and so he was wanted at the hospital. He'd need a scan, and an endoscopy: it was explained to him that a camera on a flexible tube would be passed through his mouth into what they called his 'food pipe'. Food pipe, he thought, as if he wouldn't know what an oesophagus was, why did these people think every sickness caused symptoms of infancy – he prepared a bowl of instant porridge with golden syrup, spilled oats on the countertop, and ate half the portion in his armchair. On the patio the red geraniums were still in bloom, and the grass hadn't yet been cut. A basket of stamps – issued over the course of twenty years but still, as he liked to remind me, perfectly valid – was within reach on the brown tiles of the heavy coffee table: there were birthday cards to post, but for some reason he'd had difficulty calculating the correct postage, and for the moment had given up. The endoscopy was scheduled for the following week, and he could be sedated or not, as he chose. Twelve years previously, in a small Essex hospital, he'd had a hip replaced under sedation. The surgery itself had been interesting and even amusing, and he liked to recount with his shy laugh how peculiar and in fact how funny it had been to hear the surgeon's hammer rapping away against his old hip and then, with a startlingly different sound, against the new one. But he'd disliked the sedation and the groggy twilight that followed, and called Robert to say that he would manage this procedure without: he didn't want to be messed about with, and besides, he'd be home quicker that way, and could catch up on *Countdown*.

This appointment was in a new building set apart from the main hospital: a brick limbo for souls who weren't yet damned to the wards, but had departed the world of blithe spirits untroubled by persistent coughs or bloodied toilet paper, and who could still tolerate the taste of peas. It occurred to David that really there was no reason why he couldn't take himself to hospital – the difficulty after all was with his food pipe, not with his brain – but he'd puzzled over the letter summoning him to the hospital for days, because it had been such a difficult letter to make sense of, with paragraphs he scrutinised as if they were equations that wouldn't come out right. Three times he'd phoned Robert and gone over the letter carefully, to ensure he didn't turn up in the wrong place at the wrong time, and get himself in trouble; so he conceded that driving was for the moment beyond him, and asked for help. But then Robert wanted to help, he always did; and David remembered the boy's first car, which he'd chosen because the passenger door opened wide enough to allow his mother to get in and out without straining joints wrecked by rheumatoid arthritis. And he thought then how, even after Jenny had died, her son had gone on buying cars that could have accommodated her, as if she might return one afternoon and need driving to Basildon Library to collect the audiobooks which, as she always put it, she listened to in her ears.

When the day of the appointment came, David put every document and letter he felt he might need into a Morrisons plastic bag, which he took everywhere with him in the days that followed, until the handles were crushed almost beyond use. Driving to the new building at the hospital the men talked about the weather (colder and more overcast than it ought to have been, they thought, so it was amazing how the red geraniums just went on and on), and about the new job Robert was starting soon. This would require a commute down the

Acle Straight, an undeviating carriageway infamous for fatal accidents, and which in the summer could be an eerie affair, since each year the Halvergate Marshes on either side – had David ever seen this? Yes, of course he had – became heavily populated with swans. David was cheerful enough: if he claimed a dim view of doctors in general, he was a biddable patient, and grateful at last to be solving the mystery of the muddle he'd got himself in. They found the waiting room not yet given in to the dilapidation of the hospital's main building – no scuffing on the vinyl floor, no ceiling stained by corroded pipes – and the wait itself was brief. When David's name was called he went towards the smiling, competent strangers who'd been expecting him, and felt himself grow willingly submissive. The room was bright and warm, and he noticed that many of the things in there were blue – the roll of paper that covered the trolley he lay on, the nurses' thin disposable aprons, their gloves which seemed too tight at the knuckle and too loose at the wrist. And what a relief it was to submit: to do as they asked, to repeat his name and date of birth, to lie exactly as they told him to lie (though this was difficult, because lately he'd taken to sleeping curled on his left side, as he imagined he might have done when he was a child). And the procedure in the end was no trouble to a man who'd once heard the surgeon's hammer break his own bones, and laughed about it later; only it did seem strange that a camera could pass down the oesophagus when there were days it was all he could do to drink a glass of milk. It struck him that perhaps the cause of his difficulty was a passing inflammation of some kind, or possibly even that it was psychological; and when he returned to Robert – who all that time had been bent over his phone, making notes he wouldn't look at for years – his spirits were no worse than they might have been on any other dreary afternoon when he would rather have been home.

Then there was another wait, on comfortable chairs that were also blue; and during this time David's spirits began slowly to be depleted, and he sat without speaking, and looking at the floor between his feet. Uneasily he imagined himself being anatomised and discussed, and certain conclusions being reached that he could do nothing to influence or amend. There was the sense that the walls of the waiting room were improbably lined with doors, each concealing long narrow corridors he couldn't see – that one door might lead perhaps to a course of steroids, or an antibiotic – this corridor mercifully short, and no trouble to walk down; that another might lead to a diagnosis of the nerves to which his family was prone, and immediate release from this limbo to the upper world, and to the puzzle book waiting on the coffee table with its pages folded down. But equally – set, say, in the furthest wall, and seeming no different from the others – there might be a door leading to months or even years of being, as he put it to himself, messed about with, until he was removed so far from himself that he'd no longer bother with his stamps, his copy of the *Antiques Gazette*, the birthdays on the calendar. So he waited without speaking for someone to come and direct him to the way allotted to him, and which he could not avoid. Then someone did come, and took him with Robert to a room that had nothing medical in it, as if they'd taken a wrong turn into a bewildered solicitor's office. The sun had come out, the blinds were up: everything in there was bright and clear, with no sign that anyone before them had ever taken those chairs, that desk. At the desk a small man of perhaps Robert's age spoke quite breezily as they came in – could David confirm his name, his address, his date of birth? He could, and did: it would hardly do to be sent through the wrong door – he had the Morrisons plastic bag in his lap.

'Mr Perry,' said the doctor, with no lessening of his cheerful manner, 'your endoscopy has shown a growth. There is something there. We took a biopsy,' he said (David was grateful he didn't explain what this was; that he still looked, for the moment, like a man with the intelligence of the well), 'and that will give us the final word. But it does look like cancer.' His manner was unchanged. It was merely a statement of fact: he might have been identifying a common bird.

'Oh,' said David, 'right,' and didn't look at his son, but out through the new window with its new blinds to the car park steadily filling. 'Right,' he said.

'We can't really know,' said the doctor, 'not for certain, until we have the results of the biopsy. Then we can make a plan. But it does look like it.'

Cancer, thought David. There we are – or there we possibly are: they know, but they don't know; they've said it, but they can't say it yet. On the whole, he thought, he'd have preferred certainty; but in the chapels in Yarmouth and Basildon and Norwich where he'd worshipped all his life, he'd often heard it said – and had said it as often himself – that he was in the Lord's hands. That was encouraging, he thought, very encouraging (Robert had said nothing), and he was in the Lord's hands now as he'd also been when he was a boy, and his shin splints had caused him to hobble to school, and when Jenny's father had gone missing one winter in the Basildon streets, and when Jenny had died three days after admission to hospital with a chest infection that had gone unnoticed for weeks. The prophet Isaiah, he thought, had been given a message from God eight hundred years before a new star rose over Bethlehem, and now it was handed down from Jerusalem through Wycliffe and Tyndale until it arrived in this clinic, in this small room that still smelt of fresh plaster: 'For I the Lord thy God will hold thy right hand, saying unto thee, Fear not; I will help thee.'

Because of that right hand, and because they were Englishmen, and because it had never really been their habit to discuss what they felt and feared, David and Robert left the clinic talking only briefly about what the breezy doctor had said – they knew, but they didn't know, that was the funny thing: it might not be cancer after all, they'd have to wait and see – and there was no question that David required any help that evening beyond being seen over his own doorstep, with the handshake which was the only sign of physical affection he ever shared with his son. He closed the front door behind him, and thought of changing into clean pyjamas printed with blue hibiscus flowers, of making instant hot chocolate and finishing a sudoku puzzle (though he felt that these days they seemed to be making them more and more difficult, as if motivated by spite). But before turning to the puzzle it struck him that it was never a bad thing for a man to get his affairs in order, even if it was still unclear which door had been opened to him, or how dark and short the passage was behind it. So he took the birthday calendar from the kitchen wall, and carefully – really, he thought, his bad handwriting had never been as bad as this – he wrote on the final page the passwords to his various bank accounts, his insurance policies, and the providers of his electricity, his gas and his mobile phone; then finally, in capitals, he wrote down his mother's maiden name.

A long time ago, having said all my life that I never wanted a baby, that I couldn't fathom why any free woman would do such a thing to her body and her mind, I suddenly and passionately wanted a child. I remember where I was when this feeling, so heretical to me, arrived: it was early morning, and having come down Fleet Street on my way to work I was standing at the till of a newsagent's to pay for Diet Coke, a flapjack, and a pack of Silk Cut. There were no children there, and no pregnant women; nothing had been said or done to change my mind. It had simply landed on me, and more or less immediately – because I've never known how to control an impulse, and because I was thirty, which seemed to me then a great age – we set about trying to have a child. When for some months nothing happened, I turned to the websites where women who've never met scrutinise their bodies for signs of pregnancy or fertility or miscarriage, and my vocabulary changed. I became able to communicate in acronyms impenetrable to anyone who hadn't held a dozen ovulation sticks in a dozen urine streams, and it was all so long ago that I only remember one: 2WW. I took it at first to be some dry reference to the Second World War, since they did seem to be always in battle, these women, or in flight – but in fact it refers to the 'two-week wait', the fearful, hopeful days between sex and ovulation, and the first signs the uterus had succeeded or failed (that these signs can be identical sometimes invokes a kind of madness, to which I also briefly succumbed).

That was fifteen years ago, and though I look back bewildered at that absolute but temporary change in my character, the phrase 'two-week wait' has ever since contained the memory of a particular year or so in my life – of being young, though having no idea how young; of living in a bright flat in Hackney and sometimes going to clubs where my long skirts and boy's boots must have looked absurd; of conceiving a child that would be David's first and only grandchild, then quickly losing it, and accepting soon after this loss that in fact I'd never be a mother. But now the phrase has another meaning, because we encountered the NHS policy of leaving patients with suspected cancer for no longer than two weeks before seeing a specialist; and until recently 'Two-Week Wait' was the accepted term, printed on pastel-coloured leaflets in shabby waiting rooms, or in easily comprehensible sans serif type on the NHS website. David's two-week wait began as Robert drove him home to the bungalow, and ticked away as he put the kettle on, blotted his calendar with savage black marks, phoned friends and family members to give them news that was not quite news, because it would be two weeks before the possible became certain. Now the two things have got muddled up for me, and I think of them as having more in common than in dispute – fourteen days until signs of life, or the possibility of life; fourteen days until signs of death, or the possibility of death. And in the many fortnights since then, it has sometimes occurred to me that those days were really no different from any other days – that David and Robert and I had always lived with the possibility and even the proximity of death, and that what had changed wasn't the land, but the view.

As we waited, we spoke to friends and each other. 'I suspect there are tricky times ahead,' I told Jude, who neither agreed nor contradicted me. Our friend Harry, who'd once taught me piano, allowed me to be petulant and selfish as I complained that I had a novel to edit – that really it wasn't convenient for me, the administration and the fear, those daily journeys to the bungalow; and as I complained he prepared Robert and me a meal that he served on a beautiful block-printed tablecloth, which was very like the tablecloth I'd given David the previous

Christmas, and which he'd never used. Sam, whom I'd texted in the underpass on that dreary afternoon when we saw death in the market square, wrote often to ask how things were, with the knowledge and specificity of an oncologist, and I was grateful but unhappy, thinking I'd added myself to a daily ward round, and so become indistinguishable and dull. Friends came down from Chester to play board games and eat too much cheese, because this was a sacred ritual undertaken twice a year since we were all young, and they didn't seem to mind that we were by turns distracted and hysterical – we were all getting older, that was the thing, and this particular trouble had come to Robert first, but would come to us all in the end. David's chapel friends set up a WhatsApp group called 'How Can We Help David?', and though I was unable or unwilling to pray I'd sometimes imagine their prayers going up from their rooftops like pigeons. 'I'm afraid you'll both get very ground down,' said my father, who'd witnessed the cancer deaths of his own parents-in-law, and I was afraid of this too. I began to feel that a mirror accompanied me everywhere, and that if I turned to look I'd see my selfishness and impatience, my childish inability to drive; that it was clear to everyone, and most painfully to myself, that I wasn't equal to the task of caring.

'Yes,' my father said, 'I think you'll find it very wearing,' and so one evening – this was the eighth day of our two-week wait – I sat in my study and prepared a spreadsheet of everything we could do to make things easier for David and ourselves. He'd be all right for a few months probably, and no doubt he'd improve if only he could eat more, and eat better; but we ought to find him a cleaner, and arrange for nutritious meals to be sent to the bungalow – then in due course there were carers who could now and then pop in (we used that phrase often). One afternoon the manager of a cleaning company came to visit, and was so kind I was able to cry as she made notes on her clipboard: it would be all right, she said, they weren't just a cleaning service, they could help with his ironing and so on. In fact, she said, she had a second job working in care, and so she was used to helping families with loved ones who were very ill, and she'd find just the right person for us. When she left the house she embraced me, and I never thought I'd see her again; but ten days later – David unconscious and incapable, the puzzle books and teacups gone from the coffee table, the red geraniums finally dropping their petals – I leaned dazed against the kitchen door, watching a woman reposition him on a waterproof mattress that was a very beautiful shade of blue. And when she was done she looked at me and smiled, and said: 'So it *is* you! I thought I recognised the name.'

It was a nine-day wait, in the end; and that was something, said David, less than two weeks after all, and then we'd know exactly the nature and severity of the difficulty, and what they proposed to do about it. This last appointment happened to be on the day Robert's new job began: and wasn't that typical, we said to each other, rolling our eyes, wasn't that absolutely typical. But

I could go – wasn't I his daughter, more or less? If he became muddled as he sometimes did, I could speak for him, and make a note of what he needed to know. I couldn't drive, of course, which was increasingly a problem (and at about this time I began to have bad dreams in which Robert was lying injured on the hard shoulder of a motorway at night, and I was incapable of taking him to be helped, and ignored by every car that passed us). But 'How can we help David?', people had said; so it was arranged that the pastor at the church where David worshipped would take him to the hospital to meet me at the entrance. This pastor's name was Luther, and I last remembered seeing him when we were children, and our families sometimes attended the same services in a remote Suffolk chapel – but there was no time, in those days, to stop and think how strange it was that we should meet again under those circumstances, or to wonder where the decades had gone. After the appointment, our friend Harry would take us home; and though I found it embarrassing and diminishing to be asking so often for help, it was always given quickly and even quite carelessly, as if the helper already happened to be going that way, and no thanks were needed.

None of us felt any particular anxiety that morning (though later Robert told me how the Acle Straight had seemed longer and straighter than ever as he drove away from Norwich); by then we'd accepted that it was almost certainly cancer, that there'd be no last-minute reprieve. We began to brace ourselves for months and perhaps years of dispiriting treatments – of scans and ports and cannulas, and biopsies here and there as the disease was stalked about the terrain of his body; of chemotherapy and radiotherapy that would probably cause David to finally lose his beautiful hair – and all of it expressed in some ugly and repetitious dialect we'd never needed before. I'd often thought of my mind as a file I wanted filled with fascinating, terrible and beautiful data – of the motion of bodies in orbit, and methods of torture depicted in sixteenth-century woodcuts; of how Glenn Gould played Bach on a disintegrating dining chair, and whether the poet John Burnside had ever, really, seen an angel. Now I saw that I was required to upload data I didn't want, and was afraid would be corrupting – probably I'd have to learn what a PET scan was for example, and what change was needed for NHS car parks where you couldn't ever be certain of finding a space. We'd get ground down, that was more or less certain, but we loved him and he was our friend: we'd visit Yarmouth as often as we could before the end came, his brothers would gather round; it was not unusual to hear cancer patients say, as they adjusted their silk turbans or their soft knitted hats, that the disease had brought them closer than ever to their loved ones, and given them a precious perspective on life. And then there was David's gift of finding most things silly, so that I imagined visiting him after some procedure or other, and hearing down the corridor his *Heh! Heh! Heh!*, having been amused by something someone said as they poured orange squash from a plastic jug into a plastic cup.

Then as I stood alone outside the hospital on the day

of the appointment, death – which had receded from the Jarrolds doorway across the market square, only creeping sometimes out of the kitchen cupboards or the laundry basket or the self-service tills when we were low on milk – came quickly towards me again. I was early, and watching anxiously for David – for his white hair showing under a fraying baseball cap, for that slightly sideways-leaning gait which was a little slower these days, if nothing remarkable in a man of his age. It was dismal weather, as I recall, and I'd dressed expensively in black silk and white linen, because I'd sometimes been spoken to almost with contempt on hospital wards and in clinics, and the years had taught me that even doctors find it difficult to condescend to a woman who resembles a wealthy abbess. But my attempted composure could not withstand the sight of David inching towards me with bewildered exhaustion, his baseball cap on, the Morrisons plastic bag with his hospital paperwork clutched in his left hand. Shock struck me like a bow-wave: 'Thank you,' I said to Luther, who'd brought David from the bungalow and, as he told me later, not been permitted to park near the hospital's entrance for all that his passenger had been evidently almost too frail to walk; 'thank you' – meanwhile David seemed to me too small, as if further away than I'd taken him to be. He stood flummoxed and unsteady, not able even to greet me, only waiting there with the crumpled papers asserting that yes, he was David Perry: he was born in London at the end of the war, and raised in a small dank flat with washing drying on the courtyard lines – he took his tea with artificial sweeteners, and the doctors expected him at half past ten. 'David,' I said, cheerfully enough, 'are you all right there? Are you tired today? But that's OK, Luther brought you early – go slowly now, there's heaps and heaps of time.' I put my arm through his, and the pride I took in my physical strength vanished, because it's one thing to lift a barbell with its weights precisely balanced, and another to take charge of a human body, its matter seeming dense as steel plates, but vulnerable as the pigeons so often struck on the busy road beyond the hospital grounds. The relativity of time became no longer theoretical, but actual: the minutes began to bend themselves around the terrible magnitude of the problem – my father-in-law was dying and nobody seemed to know but me, and he couldn't walk, and I couldn't carry him; it was an hour's journey to the canopied hospital entrance where a woman stood smoking and eyeing the clouds, an hour at least, the path actually lengthening as David inched down it, holding my arm and looking at me sometimes in shocked and mute appeal. Then at last we were near enough to make out, beyond immense glass doors, women at the reception desk directing patients and their families this way and that; and from a distance of perhaps thirty yards one of these women met my eye, and 'Wheelchair,' I saw her say, with comically exaggerated movements of her mouth, 'do you need a wheelchair?' Yes, I said, oh please, yes we did, badly; she ran from behind the desk and brought it out – 'There you go, be careful' – then returned to her post. Ineptly, and tripping on my absurd black silk, I manoeuvred David into the chair: 'There,' I said, 'there we are,' trying not to betray how frightened I was, or how disbelieving.

And I did not believe it, however my senses asserted that the handles of the wheelchair were rough and worn, that I could hear David's quick shallow breath; I felt as if I were an understudy stumbling onstage, who'd never bothered to learn her lines. But when we came through the hospital doors, the wheelchair and the sight of David's head drooping to his chest no longer seemed outlandish and unreal. We'd crossed the border into the land of the sick – all around us were wheelchairs and trolleys, and families looking resolute or bored or relieved, so that suddenly it seemed quite ordinary and proper that I was wheeling the chair backwards into the lift, and scrutinising signs to bring us to the correct department on the correct floor. As we came to the waiting room David had become suspended between sleep and wakefulness, and it seemed to me that all the others there were watching us with open pity and dismay. 'There we are,' I said, embarrassed by the tone I was taking, which was soothing and competent and not my own, 'there we are, and well on time, didn't I say?' At intervals there were signs instructing patients to check in, as if for a flight. There was no possibility of David finding his letter, or of taking himself to the desk; but I felt that it would be an insult to his privacy and intelligence to prise the plastic bag from his hands and find the documents myself.

'Is it all right if I take this,' I said, 'would that be OK?' – he raised his head and seemed to signal assent, then withdrew, sighing, into his private world of exhaustion. The letter when I found it was softened and stained, because he'd read it so often and so diligently; and if the woman who took it was brisk – Name? Righto. Date of birth? – when she looked again and more carefully at me, and at David leaning helplessly against the arm of his wheelchair, she became kindly: 'All right,' she said, 'that's all OK: you go and sit down, they'll call you when they're ready.' And I wonder now if some message was passed on behind the reception desk and down the corridors behind it, because we were never called: after a brief time a tall lean man, self-possessed and grave, came out to find us. He was perhaps sixty, in dark suit trousers and a white shirt. I noticed that he wore a lanyard, but had put his identification card in his breast pocket, I suppose to prevent it getting in the way if he stooped to examine a patient, and I wondered if that was hospital policy or some thoughtfulness of his own. Immediately he located David among the others waiting, and came with his hands outstretched, introducing himself: he was a gastrointestinal consultant, and he was pleased to meet us both. When I stood and tried clumsily to remove the brakes from the wheelchair, he said, 'No, please, I can do that,' and took David from me down the pale hall. I followed, and thought as I often did what a charged and peculiar relation there is between a doctor and their patient, and of how no other occupation entailed acts of service that sometimes resembled love, all carried out with such an extraordinary asymmetry of power. Later, when I recounted the day's events to Robert at home, I said how remarkable it had seemed that a consultant – an actual consultant, mind you, the title alone inspiring deference and submission together with dread, because nobody ever wanted to need a consultant, not really – had come out to meet us, and had taken the wheelchair himself.

The room he took us to was small, because it was full. A young nurse and an older one were waiting by the desk. A chair had evidently been moved to a far corner to permit the wheelchair; another was waiting for me. The nurses introduced themselves with so exact an echo of the consultant's courteous kindliness that I wondered if they'd rehearsed together before we entered, and I smiled and thanked them with gratitude deepened by fear. Then David – because he was roused by the lights or the significance of the occasion, or because there was a change in some chemical process affecting his cognition – sat straighter in his chair, nodded and smiled at them all, and said with a kind of gruff shyness that he was sorry, it was just that lately he'd been in a bit of a muddle.

The consultant at his desk, leaning towards us with hands loosely clasped, said: 'Thank you for coming today, Mr Perry, especially as I can see you're feeling poorly. And you are his daughter?'

'Yes,' I said. 'Well, I'm his daughter-in-law.'

'I understand,' he said. 'Now Mr Perry, I think you're aware there was an abnormality in your oesophagus – in your food pipe, that is. And we've taken a look, and I can tell you that there is a growth there. This is why you're having difficulty swallowing, and why you've been feeling so unwell.' I saw then on David's face a lively, curious expression which was familiar, and absolutely his own: almost a smile, and almost a shrug – a resigned, good-humoured and faintly irritated acceptance of the way things were. 'Well,' he said. 'Well, we did think so, didn't we?'

'We can see from the scan there are other changes in your body too – in your bones, and in your brain. And although we could operate on your food pipe, we wouldn't be able to operate on those other places.' He paused, I suppose to establish that we understood the significance of what he'd said; and it didn't strike me until the following day that there'd been no bald reference to tumours, grades, metastases: the language was almost abstract, though its meaning was particular. It was as if merely the word 'cancer' possessed for him some malign power, or brought with it a kind of public shame. In her memoir *Love's Work*, the philosopher Gillian Rose – who died at forty-eight of a cancer that began in her ovaries – writes: 'For you, "cancer" means, on the one hand, a lump, a species of discrete matter with multiplying properties, on the other hand, a judgement, a species of ineluctable condemnation.' I wonder now if the consultant had felt, in some unreasoning part of his admirably educated mind, that David's condemnation came not from the tumour, but from speaking the word aloud.

And in fact it was never a doctor that spoke explicitly with us about the nature of this cancer, but an undertaker, who – nine days later, almost to the hour – sat with us at David's kitchen table drinking tea. 'I knew a young woman who had it,' he said. 'Oh, I can't tell you, it was a terrible time. The tumour and the oesophagus grew around each other like the double helix in a strand of DNA. It became tighter and tighter, and when they passed a pipe down so that she could eat, the tumour attached itself to the pipe. So you know it could never be taken out, because it had become part of her. This was better,' he said, gesturing behind him to the sitting room where David had watched *Countdown*, and where he now lay with a small cross, carved from olive wood, resting on the blanket that covered him. 'It might not have been better for you, but it was better for him.' And a little later, because we enjoyed the undertaker's company and wanted to keep him with us, he explained how in Christian tradition bodies were buried facing east, so that at the Day of Judgement they'd rise to face Christ coming with the morning sun – but that ministers were buried facing the church, not allowed a day off even when they were heading for the marriage supper of the Lamb.

'Now,' said the consultant, 'there are treatments beside surgery of course, but those are difficult things to endure; and just at the moment I think we'd all agree you're not quite strong enough for something along the lines of chemotherapy.' He glanced then almost deferentially at the older nurse, who nodded – 'Not now,' she said. 'No, not now.'

'He's so weak,' I said, 'that's the thing.' I'd wanted to appear clever, competent, possibly even a little grand, but my voice was high and desperate as a child's. 'I've tried and tried,' I said, wanting to assure this man and these women that I'd been good, 'but he can't eat, or he doesn't like to, and isn't that half the problem? He's starving, he isn't getting any nutrition at all.' Then I realised that for only the second time in my life I'd taken David's hand, or possibly he'd taken mine; and that I hadn't thought to do so in ten years, not since we'd stood together beside the freshly turned soil of Jenny's grave, and I'd laughed to stave off our tears and said, 'Look, can we agree that we won't do this again for a very, very long time?'

'What we would like to do, Mr Perry,' said the nurse, 'is fit a stent. That will open the food pipe and make it easier for you to eat. Then soon you'll feel much better, and you'll be able to eat all the things you like. Sometimes,' she said, turning to me and speaking confidentially, 'I've seen a stent fitted and someone make a remarkable change, really remarkable, they go on for months or years afterwards.'

'A stent,' said David, examining the word as if it were an object that had been handed to him. 'Very good. Yes, that sounds promising.' And it did sound promising – he'd see Yarmouth again, and drop fish and chip crumbs on his jacket; he'd eat pavlova on his birthday, and I'd tell him again and again that his glasses could do with a clean. 'And we can do that soon,' said the nurse – she named a date in five days' time – 'would that be convenient?'

'I should think so,' said David, looking at me as if I were the calendar on the kitchen wall. 'Yes, I should think so, I don't think I've got anything else on.'

There was a pause then, during which the consultant looked at the nurse again with his assessing deference, as if to establish that she'd said all she'd needed to say. Then he leaned forward, ran his fingers down the blue lanyard resting on his well-pressed shirt, and said: 'What we are talking about now, you see, is palliative care. Our priority now, Mr Perry, is to keep you safe.' He went on speaking for a time – the palliative-care team would eventually be in touch, we'd be given all the information we needed about the stent and so on – but I heard little of it because I was so struck by that word: that he'd been unable to promise David's comfort, only his safety.

'And I can see you have a wonderful family,' the doctor said, becoming warmer and warmer, 'I can see you're going to be taken care of.' This embarrassed both David and me; so I said that yes, he did have a wonderful family – that Robert had been a carer when he was a child and then again when I'd been ill for months, and so it all came naturally to him. 'And I'll do my best,' I said, now holding David's hand between both of mine, because he knew me very well – knew how impatient I was, and that though I lost my temper only rarely I always struggled to find it again; knew that I'd never done the decent thing and become a mother, or even learned to drive – and I wanted to reassure him that despite all this, I really was going to try.

After the appointment, Harry – who'd been waiting to take us home – came hurriedly out of his car. He'd always worn beautiful and considered clothes, and on other days when I'd been his passenger it was always because he was taking me to see some half-abandoned Saxon church with wooden angels bearing up a wooden roof, or to go and be hurled about in the shining sea among the Norfolk seals. So when I saw him, and registered the fine wool coat and the scarlet cotton square knotted in the collar, my lagging mind interpreted these images and concluded there must be some pleasure in the offing, and I was briefly happy. But these were scenes from an old life, and quickly replaced by the reality set out in a small, warm room by a man already, I imagined, being kind to someone else: David could never be made better, he could only be made safe.

'I knew immediately,' Harry told me later that same day, 'I saw it in your eyes, there was no need to ask.' So he didn't ask and we didn't tell him, not really; I remember reaching forward and holding David's shoulder through the thin cotton jacket and saying, 'Well, it's just what we thought, really, it's oesophageal cancer, but they'll fit a stent on Friday and that's going to make all the difference in the world.'

When David crossed the threshold of our house, he felt there'd been a change in the direction of the wind. He'd been in such a muddle, he thought, and been so tired; and how diminishing and strange it had been to be in the seat of a wheelchair, when in the years of his marriage he'd expertly marshalled Jenny's chair from place to place. But going down our familiar narrow hall, and turning into the familiar green room with its books and lamps, its pictures that seemed to have a habit of shifting askew on the walls when nobody was in there to see it, he felt himself rally in his body and spirits. So yes, he said, yes he'd love a cup of tea, and maybe a biscuit – he took the seat he'd always taken, stretched out legs crossed comfortably at the ankle, and sighed. When I put the Morrisons plastic bag out into the hall, he thought how good it was to have it gone from his sight; and also how good it was to be released from that bluish hospital light, in which the dark spots lately mottling the backs of his hands had taken on the look of symptoms of the plague or some other antique sickness. For some time he examined the room as if establishing that, yes, it did seem as if he'd die rather short of the national average; but there, still, was the coffee table Robert had made, there was the quilt worn out by dogs who never could be persuaded down from the sofa – there was the fireplace, which had often called to mind his grandfather setting fire to the chimney and congratulating himself on the shilling saved. The world went steadily on, and he went steadily with it – was not about to be hurled off, having lost his purchase; and when I brought him tea he was able to rest it on the swell of his stomach, because you see he hadn't got so thin as all that. Then one of the dogs came to rest her head on his knee, and this was so unusual it occurred to him that possibly she was getting old and frail, and needed his comfort – 'All right there, Janey,' he said, 'all right'; and meanwhile Ruby, our fox-coloured saluki who could never bear to see love offered elsewhere, watched jealously from across the room.

    When I came in not with tea but with red wine, I

saw with bewildered gratitude that he seemed himself again – smiling at Janey, petting her with a kind of distracted affection; sitting more or less upright, and giving me that look so characteristic of him, which was partly good-humoured, and partly a little exasperated by the trouble the business was giving him; but there was no self-pity, no objections to some injustice of providence. Though a man of faith, he'd have got on well enough with the conscientious atheist Christopher Hitchens, who having received his own diagnosis of oesophageal cancer wrote, 'To the dumb question "why me?" the cosmos barely bothers to return the reply: why not?'

'Well,' I said – but what tone do you take with a man unlikely to see the Christmas after next, when it's already autumn? 'Oh, David. But really I think we knew.'

'Yes,' said David (and we were each so measured that it was only Janey, sighing in her sleep, who showed signs of sorrow). 'You know you're going to die eventually,' he said. 'But I didn't think it would be so soon.'

I wanted to say that 'soon' had no meaning or duration – that Robert would be home soon, that my birthday was soon, that my hair was going grey and soon would be as white as his. Long before I was born, my grandfather had died eight months after cancer was found in his pancreas, and that had been very soon, because they'd promised him ten – but in two years' time I hoped to see for the first time a total eclipse of the sun, and that was also soon.

'Then again,' I said, 'you might be hit by a car next week, or I might.'

'*Heh! Heh!* That's true!'

'It is all sooner than we thought, I know. But they'll fit this stent, you'll be eating again, it'll make all the difference. Remember what the nurse said? It'll make all the difference in the world.'

'You needn't worry about money,' he said then, grinning as if confiding a secret. 'I haven't spoken to Robert about this, he doesn't like it. But there's more than enough.'

'Wonderful,' I said, raising my glass, toasting his prudence and his foresight. 'Whatever care you need, we can get it. Let's get you a robot butler: Robert has always wanted one of those, ever since he was a boy.' And yes, he said, a little distracted by the thought, and not laughing as I'd hoped he might; because that hadn't been what he'd meant, not really, and he wasn't certain if he should say: I'm not talking about what I need. I'm talking about what I leave behind.

Many months later, going with the dogs through a silent and iron-cold winter day, Robert asked me if I knew of Plato's disagreement with the miserable philosopher Diogenes about the essential nature of reality, which had had something to do with the cup-ness of a cup, and the table-ness of a table. Diogenes the Cynic, who they say lived for a time in a clay container for wine, had had no patience with Plato's abstractions and his assertion that the essence of a cup, for example, lay not in the thing itself, but in a perfect idea of cup-ness that preceded the making of all cups. 'I can see this cup,' Diogenes said, 'I'll give you that. But where, I ask you, is the cup-ness?'; and so the men bickered back and forth to entertain themselves. When I remember that evening – how David petted Janey and wondered aloud whom to phone first with the news; of how we made each other laugh – I think of his unchanging and essential David-ness. 'He isn't himself,' we'd say, or 'He seems himself again,' but really I had always felt his David-ness was visible, if only just. Even listing with exhaustion in his wheelchair in that small consultant's office, the looks he'd given the doctor, and had exchanged with me, had all been essentially his own – humorous and resigned; faintly irritated, but always disinclined to complain. I thought, too, of the last we'd ever seen of Jenny, who – ten years before, and in the summer – had been admitted to an Essex hospital ward having developed a curious panting style of breathing which had baffled the asthma nurse. For months, as it turned out, she'd had a chest infection, and this had gone unnoticed because she'd been disabled by rheumatoid arthritis for so long, and so depleted by decades of medication, that the symptoms of this new disease had gone unremarked among her general exhaustion, and her tendency to be both hot and chilled. When we visited her on the ward, we found a catheter had been fitted, and a dispiriting trickle of urine accumulating in a vessel marked with units of volume. The meagre quantity of liquid in the bottle concerned the nurses, and seemed also to trouble a doctor who became condescending and irritated when I asked what was happening, and what he thought they could do – 'I've already explained once,' he'd said, 'I'm sure I don't need to do it again.' On the third day of her hospital stay, which was also the last day of her life, her manner had been no different from any other day: cheerful, with the skilled good cheer a person can develop after a lifetime of disability, and rather bossy in the way of a woman who has a husband and a son to keep in line. Sending us home – a nurse was coming to take blood, we'd only be a nuisance – she'd instructed David in stage whispers to ensure we had twenty pounds for the cab. Then 'I love you all,' she'd said; and as we reached the door blew us a kiss. But because it had been many years since she could raise a hand to her face, she'd done this with quick sideways turns of her head, hurling kisses from her mouth towards us – as she'd always done, a constituent part of her Jenny-ness, and the last we had of it.

And when Robert came home that evening, he found his father and his wife essentially themselves, more or less. We hadn't wept or embraced or raged – that would have been embarrassing, and not in our natures, or the nature of our relation to each other. It hadn't occurred to me to pray, for example, or to be any more pious than comes naturally to me; and David had been garrulous in his own particular distracted way, and often chuckling to himself. And when we gave Robert the news, he too maintained his essential Robert-ness – no anger, no bitter sense that God or systems or individuals had failed, and were to blame for such an unjust state of affairs. He was quiet and considered, accepting what we'd been told with an expression that was sometimes frowning and sometimes illuminated with hope – would he really be able to eat again? Was that really what she'd said? But now I wonder whether I saw this because I had a perfect, preceding idea of Robert's gentle intelligent assessment of the world, and that because of this I failed to see the loss already opening out in him, relentless as a breach between tectonic plates.

David wanted to go home. When pressed to stay, to have a comfortable bed made up in my study so that he needn't bother with the stairs, he felt himself become a little irritated – he had a home of his own, which had no stairs to bother him – the kettle and the jar of hot chocolate were easily within reach, the winter almond was flowering over the lawn beyond the kitchen window; probably there was more post that needed his attention, and he may have missed calls from friends troubled he'd not been seen in chapel for a week or two. The awful muddle he'd got himself in that morning had passed, and he couldn't account for it, but certainly there was no need now for a wheelchair, or even to be helped out of the sofa where Janey, her anxious black eyes fogged with cataracts, was watching him prepare to leave. He put on his cotton jacket and his baseball cap, and took up the Morrisons plastic bag; he embraced me quickly, saying that yes, please, he'd see me in the morning, if that was all right, and then perhaps Robert would visit after work? Of course he would. All afternoon and evening he'd talked, so that on the journey home he felt he'd run out of himself, only saying he liked the Christmas lights that were beginning to appear, and which had been wrapped unevenly around the lamp posts on the street where he lived. When Robert drew up outside the bungalow, David saw his own car on the drive, and couldn't think when he'd last been at the wheel, or when he'd use it again – in fact it seemed bizarre that he could ever have managed to captain that enormous and bewildering vessel through the streets. And how odd it was (Robert's hand was at his elbow; they were beside the bank of lavender he really should cut back), this change in his capacity, when all his life he'd been in the driver's seat, taking Jenny to the library or the hospital, or up to Yarmouth when the weather was good and the boy sat unspeaking behind him in the passenger seat trying not to be sick. Now they were going together down the hall, over cheap mats he'd put down because our dogs disliked the cold hard tiles on the floor; and yes, he said, it would be useful if Robert could make a hot drink and take him through to the bedroom – though of course he didn't need undressing, there was no need for that. 'All right then,' they said to each other, 'all right?', parting on the handshake that had always been the pact of affection between them, when David was best man for Robert at our wedding for example, or when Jenny was buried and we'd all agreed not to subject each other to grief for a good long while, if it could be helped.

Then he sat for a time on the edge of the bed. Nothing troubling or even unfamiliar now in sight – no wheelchair, no grave stranger concluding the two-week allotted span with vague but definite news; no hospital signage in that curious, flat NHS blue. There was his clock radio, which was not dirty precisely, only greased with the deposits of his life – there was the chest of drawers in varnished pine containing his pyjamas and socks and pants, and resting on it were the books he liked to keep near at hand, with his Bible the nearest of these. The people who'd lived in the bungalow before him had been young, and papered the wall with scenes of a jungle in which parrots peered astutely out between fronds of improbable foliage – 'I'll change that,' he often said, 'that'll have to come down,' but secretly he liked it, because he found it funny. Robert had drawn the curtains, and streetlight showed faintly through them. There was a mug of sweet tea cooling beside the clock radio, and he ought to drink it; his pyjamas were stuffed under his pillow, and he ought to put them on. But it had been a long day, and there were other long days coming – though 'Fear not,' God had told the prophet in Jerusalem, 'I will help thee.' Carefully – because his body now seemed to demand as much skill and attention as a vehicle did, to be moved from one place to another – he lay down, thinking how often he'd heard it said that 'fear not' was the phrase that occurred most often in scripture – 365 times, in fact, once for each day of the year, which was either a coincidence or a marvellous piece of design. Too late for tea now, that had long gone cold – but there on the cabinet beside the clock radio was the latest copy of the *Antiques Gazette*, and lately there'd been no time to take a look. What a treat, he thought, it had never failed him – that amusing catalogue of spoiled porcelain dogs in their porcelain ribbons, punch bowls in chased silver as large as tin baths, mangy teddy bears for which some fool somewhere would part with a queen's ransom – he reached for it.

~

Shortly before we left London for Norwich – ran away, as I often put it, because we'd bolted at short notice and with relieved glee – I met a woman with a shaved head at a wedding in Yorkshire. At this wedding I really knew only the bride; and because I can never see a crowd of strangers without scanning it for love, I passed that weekend looking for someone for whom I'd feel that instant loyal intimacy that strikes me every few years. Towards the end of the evening, as I stood in my home-made dress of blue silk watching other guests dancing or tending to an immense fire, the bride came to fetch me and said there was someone I must meet, since she lived not far from Norwich, and I was going to be in need of friends. When we were introduced I understood at once, and without evidence, that I'd know this woman in my middle and old age and my dotage: her name was Sally, and she was taller than me by far; her head was shaved almost to the scalp, and the fair bristles glinted in the firelight. She wore a blue tapestry coat that I suppose was made in the sixties, and though she never wears it now I see it often, since it hangs on the back of the door to the room in her house where Robert and I sometimes sleep. And because I've never really believed that time consists of one thing after another, I wonder now if what I felt for her then was informed by a backwards echo of the coming years – that it was in fact a well-earned affection, because already we'd made each other meals when we were heartbroken or sick, already drunk and smoked too much in various small towns; and because already, and in ten years' time, she'd come to my house early one morning in autumn, and driven me to David's bungalow the morning after his appointment.

On this drive she was cheerful, practical, bolstering, which has always been her nature: we were all coming to an age when parents needed more care, that was the thing, and of course the diagnosis would take time to sink in, that was only natural. But we had to remember we weren't alone – they'd send carers when the time came, Macmillan nurses and so on (people always said they were saints, didn't they? Absolute saints); give it a few weeks and it would become normal, one can get used to anything. Her hair in those days was longer, and dyed fuchsia pink – there was music on the radio, and everything about her and about the car insisted on life, and refused death: the skim of fur left by dogs, evidence of lifts given to her sons and friends, tubes of lipstick, house keys, scarlet hair-ties, books, paperwork, everything so ordinary and vital that it fended off the memory of moving through the hospital with David, and of how sometimes he lifted his head from his shoulder and looked at me with an expression of wordless shock. So when we came to the bungalow I kissed and thanked her and said, with doubting attempts at courage, that yes, really it would be all right – I'd put the kettle on, make porridge possibly, he always seemed able to eat that. 'Go on,' she said, 'go on in, and good luck. It's all going to be OK.'

The door of the bungalow was unlocked. I went in. It was a bright clear day, and light came like a weakening torch-beam through the kitchen and down the narrow hall. There at once was the smell I'd associated with David since I was sixteen, and first visited the house in Basildon to see the boy I loved: this smell a little sour from the cleaning products he'd always used, and sweet from the steam that rose from the endless cups of tea and instant coffee he drank through the day. I called out *cooee*, which I'd never done before and have never done since, but which I suppose I'd remembered from when I was a child, and my mother would announce herself in this way when visiting elderly neighbours who'd never got in the habit of locking their doors. There was no reply. That troubled me. I stood alone in the silence, and this did not consist only of the absence of the radio on the kitchen windowsill, or of some morning television playing in the living room – it was worse than that. I understood there was no hope I'd hear the toilet flush, or a grunt as David struggled from the worn seat of his armchair with his shy, pleased smile: it was silence that had weight and matter, and I moved through it with difficulty. David's bedroom door was open four steps from where I stood, and represented an impassable territory unmarked on any map. It didn't occur to me, standing in that awful substantial quiet, that he was dead. It occurred to me that he was suffering and lonely, and that this was our fault, who loved him best: we ought never to have let him go home. And though there's nothing wrong with my heart — not, at any rate, the heart that consists of muscle and valve — the disease I've had since my thirties has left it skittish, and it often wakes me in the small hours knocking like something has been locked out. Standing there, that troublesome old knock began — *little pig, little pig, let me come in!* — and it was days before I felt it relent, though I couldn't tell you whether that was because something had entered, or had given up and gone away.

After a time I went in. The bedside lamp was on. The numbers on the old clock radio were red: I didn't register the time. The curtains — which only weeks before David had bought from a local seamstress, and proudly showed us the day they were hung — were still closed. He lay across the bed at a curious angle which at the time I could not understand: on his side, his legs drawn slightly up towards his stomach. He still had on the shirt and tracksuit trousers he'd worn to the hospital, and the shirt had ridden up to show a reach of hairless skin that was very pale over his broad bent back. His white hair was flattened and splayed on the pillow, and he held a rolled-up copy of the *Antiques Gazette* like a child consoling himself with a favourite toy. I'd been afraid to begin with, and now I was ashamed: this was an affront to his dignity, I should have knocked on the bedroom door. Seeing me, he made a noise of pleasure and surprise and with great effort began to reposition himself on the mattress to greet me; but his body was stiff, and he found it difficult to raise his head. I sat on the edge of the bed and reached for his hand, and then – concealing my fear with a nannyish, chiding tone I disliked – asked what on earth he was still doing in bed at that late hour, that it was really most unlike him. Then I made a comical show of relenting – 'Ah, you just stay here, Dad,' I said. 'Just lie down a little longer, I'll put the kettle on.' I'd been his daughter-in-law for twenty-two years, but never called him 'Dad', because this would outrage my attachment to truth – he was not my father: my father lived in the West Midlands, and collected clocks that were almost past repair. But I noticed then that quite naturally I was calling him Dad, and wondered if this had begun the day I understood we'd lose him: 'It's all right, Dad,' I said, 'I'll get you tea, you stay where you are.'

'I'm being a bother,' he said. He seemed not to want to let go of my hand. 'I've been in a bit of a muddle.'

Then I looked down at the carpet, and saw it was stained with liquid that had dribbled from the bed to the bathroom, and in that moment the vague understanding that for weeks had attended me like a melody I'd overheard and couldn't forget was replaced at last, and irreversibly, with certainty. For weeks Robert and I had swung between that first unwelcome prophecy – *this is all very well, but he is dead* – and the persuasive cheerfulness of friends and professionals: you'll get ground down, but one can get used to anything, and when he can eat again it'll make a difference, it'll make all the difference in the world. Horribly, it occurred to me to be vindicated – we'd been right all along, we'd seen death in the market square: hadn't I told them? Didn't we say? He wouldn't let go of the *Antiques Gazette*, and that was death; he hadn't thought to pull down his shirt to cover himself, and that was death; death in the urine stain on the carpet, death in the fond apologetic way he returned my clasp, death in the pale skin forming on the tea left untouched by the bed. The door to his bedroom had not been set in a wall perpendicular to the floor, it had been an open hatch at my feet: I was falling now after David who'd been falling for some time, and soon Robert would be falling with us. In the narrow gap between the curtains, the ordinary world turned on – weeds were fringing the artificial lawn, and a neighbour was hanging out her washing on this one fine day; I heard the passing buses that were busy because Christmas shopping had begun – but that was all remote and unreachable as the patch of sky viewed from the bottom of a well. So here we are, I thought: he was dying, and doing it quickly – there'd be weeks ahead, not months; no time, as my father had said, to be ground down. But what could have prepared me for the urine stains on the carpet, for the frail body which seemed overnight to have dwindled down still further, so that I thought of how the carcase of a fox or deer will be picked clean by insects? 'It'll be all right,' I said, but in fact I had no idea what I ought to do, and I think now with shame of how impossible it seemed that I could phone Robert then, because it was the second day of his new job, and all our lives – just like David – we'd lived in fear of inconveniencing others, of being found to have erred in some way.

I wanted to be out of the room – to reach, if for the final time, that bright circle of ordinary life diminishing overhead. 'I'll be just a moment,' I said, 'I'll be back soon'; I pulled my hand from David's and ran from the bungalow past the lawn that would never be weeded, the lavender that would never be cut back, and saw Sally's car still on the verge. The lights were on, she was ready to go – I thumped the passenger window and pleaded with her to stay, to come in. I was wringing my hands with a gesture I knew was theatrical but which I couldn't help: 'Sally,' I said, 'I think something's wrong, he's so much worse than they said. Can you come in, I can't do it on my own, will you come in and see?' What I needed was a witness, to prove that after all I'd not gone mad – was not summoning out of my writer's imagination a tall tale in which I was a seer, and all my doubters fools. And when she came in with me, I saw with gratitude that she too was shocked (though, as eventually she told me, she'd never for a moment thought it would be days before the undertaker came). 'Dad,' I said – his back was still exposed, and this was not quite decent, and so I understood I'd failed him again – 'this is my friend Sally. She's just come to say hello. She's just come to help us a bit.'

Then there was a wry, pleased nod that contained his David-ness: 'Sorry about all this,' he said, 'I'm being a bit of a bother.' And no, we said – we'd each taken an arm to bring him seated against the headboard of the bed, while the parrots on the wall drew nearer in disinterested curiosity – no, of course not, it wasn't a bother at all.

'Well it is a bit,' he said, contradicting me with sudden lively precision, in the way he'd contradict me about the wisdom of an assisted dying bill, for example, or denouncing Gordon Brown (mysteriously, given his lifelong Labour sympathies) as a miserable Scottish nark, 'it is a bit of a bother.' When with difficulty we had him seated, and his mottled hands were resting on the fading floral quilt, Sally followed me out to the kitchen, and having moved beyond David's hearing I spoke in a childish querulous way I heard, disliked, and could do nothing to prevent: 'What should I do? Nobody's coming, not yet – the hospital is sending a letter to his doctor, the palliative-care team will be told – but nobody told me when. He can't walk, Sally, I don't think he made it to the bathroom in time.'

'It's going to be all right,' she said – she was Julian of Norwich, and all manner of things would be well – 'but he is obviously weak, and I think you should call his GP.' Then we laughed at ourselves, because of course we understood that no GP could be found, these days, without entering a hopeless morning lottery administered by receptionists taken aback at the folly of acquiring tonsillitis, or a tender and troubling lump. 'But this is different,' she said, 'it will be on his records, somebody will come.' Then because I'd already made her late, and because receding shock revealed more courage than I thought I had, I sent her away. The door closed behind her, and mercifully there was a breach in the silence: movement in the bedroom, of a teaspoon rattling in a mug, a quilt shifting restlessly over a sheet – and oh, he's still with us, I thought, beginning by now to find myself absurd, he's not dead yet! I'd become frightened of him, and ashamed of my fear; I discovered that going into the bedroom required me to set my shoulders and resolve as if I were walking into the wind. But there he was, drinking his tea a little noisily, in the way that for most of my life had irritated me, but which now struck me as defiant; so I sat on the edge of the bed and asked how he was.

'I just don't feel right,' he said.

'Do you have any pain?'

'No, I just don't feel right. I needed the toilet in the night but I had trouble, I couldn't get there in time, not really.'

'That's OK,' I said, 'I'll clean that up. But I think I should call the doctor, I think someone should come. Things are changing, aren't they?'

'There isn't any pain, no pain at all. I just don't feel right. I haven't felt right for a long time, really.'

I was holding his hand again. 'Robert will be here before we know it,' I said. 'But I'm going to call the doctor now. Shall we see if somebody can come?'

Out in the kitchen there was an oval dining table in cheap pine, its yellowed varnish rubbed thin from the press of David's elbows where he always sat. It had come from the old house in Basildon, which was not far from where his parents had lived, and where – before the custom changed – he'd sometimes sat with Jenny on the patch of lawn beyond the front door and greeted neighbours passing by. On this table he'd written his birthday cards, and sorted his many thousand stamps into packets, and listened to the *Test Match Special* over many cups of sweetened tea; Robert had sometimes been set there when he was an infant, and Jenny had persuaded his small insistent limbs into clothes she'd made before her hands became too stiff and swollen for her knitting needles. David hadn't been certain it would fit in the bungalow's kitchen with its view of the flowering almond, but it had just slipped in between the window and the door – so he'd taken up his position again. The philosopher–poet Lucretius, in his work *On the Nature of Things*, saw the world and everything in it as composed of indivisible atoms, which might be worn away or transferred from one thing to another – a statue depleted by repeated kisses for example, or a stone diminished by the flow of water. So when I sat at that table to make my first call for help, resting my arms on its worn and flaking varnish, I imagined it still containing particles dislodged through time from David's life, and the lives of his wife and his son: of birthday cake, antiseptic cream, Avon perfume, French cheese tentatively chosen for special occasions, ink pressed through the page of Robert's homework, the sweet German wine David only ever bought at Christmas – all of it present and persisting – all of it constituent parts of that afternoon.

The doctor's receptionist in the end was kinder than I'd feared she might be, and less perturbed. Oh, dear, she said, that did all sound very difficult – yes, a letter would probably soon be going out. The GP would be told. Somebody would be in touch.

'But you see, I don't think there's time,' I said. 'I don't think there's time to wait – he can't be left, I think someone needs to come.'

'Well,' said the receptionist. In the pause that followed I imagined certain concessions being made: 'I could ask the doctor to call you?'

'Thank you,' I said, 'yes please, but do you think somebody will come?' It struck me that I was asking for something outlandish. I'd only once known of a GP making a home visit, and this had been when I was fifteen, and so tormented by an abscess in the ear canal I'd vomited streaks of blood from an excess of codeine and antibiotics. This GP (who many years later, as it turned out, was to hang himself in his garage) had held my foot through the quilt and said, 'Oh dear oh dear oh dear,' and that had seemed to alleviate the pain a little. But a lifetime had intervened since then, and perhaps that was no longer the policy – 'Well,' said the receptionist, still unperturbed, 'let's see what the doctor says, shall we?'

Some time ago, in the restaurant of a hotel not far from Hexham Priory, a friend told me he was afraid I'd never allowed myself to experience anger at the most difficult events of my childhood and my life, and at those who'd held power over me and so had a hand in the difficulty. I'd been brought up to examine my actions and even my thoughts for signs of sinfulness, and never really got out of the habit; so I put down my fork and looked at him with astonishment – 'No,' I said, 'because isn't anger a sin?', and I remember the smiling exasperated expression of a man who knew me quite well, and might have predicted I'd say such a thing. And I couldn't tell you whether I've done my best to curtail the anger I do feel, because I keep trying against the odds to be good; or whether I'd said 'no' with an old reflex from the faith of my youth; or whether (naturally I prefer to think this) I simply have a nature which, as the Psalmist says of God, is slow to anger and plenteous in mercy. But I do know this – if anger is a sin, I can't think of what followed that afternoon, when a GP did in fact come to the darkening bungalow, without staining the fabric of my soul. And the sin of my anger is compounded with guilt – hadn't I stood on the doorstep in those pandemic lockdown evenings, good grateful citizen that I am, clapping until the heels of my palms were bruised? Hadn't I once, spurred on by vuvuzelas and trombones played in the terraces further up the road, gone out banging a copper saucepan with a wooden spoon? What is the British state religion, secularists that we are, but the NHS? We make sport of deploring the waiting lists for our corns and rotten tonsils and our degraded hips – but the doctors and nurses themselves, with their scrubs blue as the Virgin Mother's robes, their capable hands prone to dermatitis what with all the washing – they must be beyond reproach, or what would be the foundation of our faith? When a medic is found to have caused harm, the shock is greater than if it had been a car mechanic, or a cook; and it is certainly greater than if it had been a priest. To think she did all that, we say, and her a nurse!

The GP called while David was sleeping. Whenever I went quietly into his room with my knocking heart, I'd find him lying on his left side with his knees drawn slightly up. He never seemed able to get himself straight, or to keep his head on the pillow: his body settled over and over again into that same childlike position, and always laid diagonally across the bed. The *Antiques Gazette* had been set aside; the red numbers on the clock radio seemed to me to be changing bewilderingly fast. Time hurried: I suppose it does, when you're falling. I moved between the bedroom and the oval kitchen table, unable to put down my phone; and though I've always kept a ghoulish interest in sickness and injury it never once occurred to me to look up the nature of his cancer, or even what the fitting of a stent would involve: these things seemed incidental to the plain bare fact that a man was dying in the room down the hall. I am never lonely when I am alone, but I was lonely then – I texted Sally to thank her, I texted Robert to say that he shouldn't go home, but should come straight to the bungalow; I texted Sam, who for all I knew was at that moment going out to greet a patient with his hands outstretched, and saying no, no: he'd take the wheelchair himself. I called my mother, who perhaps felt things weren't as bad as I'd taken them to be; who reminded me, as she often had over the years, that our times were in God's hands, and I did not say (as I'd often thought of saying over the years) that since this must also have been true in times of desperate suffering I found it no consolation at all. Then – because I didn't know what help would be coming, or when – I looked online for the kind of walking frame they give to the elderly and infirm, found one in stock in the Argos in town by the river, and ordered it to be collected later that same day. And when at last the doctor called it was a woman's voice I heard, and I was glad. This was not because I really believed women essentially more compassionate than men, or less likely to think my dismay misplaced, but because that was the sort of thing I was supposed to believe. This voice was tired and brisk. Evidently I was on speakerphone: I heard paper shuffling, and other voices in other rooms.

'Yes?' she said. 'How can I help?'

'It's my father-in-law,' I said. 'Yesterday he was diagnosed with oesophageal cancer. There can't be any treatment, but soon they're going to fit a stent. But I'm concerned – he's worsened overnight. It's happening too fast, I think he's becoming incontinent. I don't know what to do, and I don't know how to help.' Sally and Jude, I thought, would never have taken that frightened and uncertain tone. They were mothers. They would have known what to do.

The doctor sighed. The irritated exhalation reached me down the line: I felt the chill movement of the air.

'All right. What's his name? His date of birth?' Now there were the sounds of tapping on a keyboard alongside the shuffling papers; 'I haven't got the letter yet,' she said. She sighed again: 'Well, really. This just keeps on happening'; and I wondered briefly if some avenging angel with a particular line in spite had passed over Norfolk that autumn, leaving women and men in bungalows and terraces waking up unable to swallow, or distractedly making peculiar black marks on their kitchen calendars.

'I'm so sorry,' I said, and I meant it. She was a doctor, and beyond reproach: no doubt her compassion had been exhausted by a long day the likes of which I couldn't conceive, what with my indolent life of reading and writing. Besides, it was scarcely her fault that David's cancer had outpaced the internal post. 'We can look after him for now,' I said – I wanted to reassure her – 'we won't leave him. But what should we do if he becomes incontinent, or there's pain? I don't think I can move him. How long before somebody comes?'

'Well, I can't come now,' she said.

'No. No, of course you can't.' I was humble then: what had I been thinking?

Then again there was the brisk movement of papers on her desk, and she read out his address: 'Is that it?'; and yes, I said, yes it was, thank you – she was so kind. 'I'll come this evening,' she said. 'All right? I'll see you then.'

It was almost dark when she came, and Robert was not yet home. I opened the door and for a moment couldn't pick her figure out of the November dusk, because she'd moved a little back from the step and seemed almost to be moving away, as if I'd taken too long to reach the door and tested her patience. 'Hello,' I said. 'Yes, hello – thank you so much'; and as she came nearer I saw that she was in late middle age, with neat grey hair and a neat body, neatly dressed. 'Mr Perry?' she said; and yes, I said, this was the right house, and we were so grateful. She came quickly in. She had with her a plastic folder of documents; the plastic was a translucent urine yellow. I'd imagined, despite her harried manner on the phone, that she'd bring with her some kindly gravity, almost like that of a woman of the cloth – that if her profession required attention to the body, it also and necessarily attended to the soul. 'He's in here,' I said, standing back to let her pass; then I watched her turn into the room with a curious quick-stepping authority, as if she'd visited often, if never out of choice. David, having heard the knock at the door, was sitting on the edge of the bed as though he wanted to appear presentable. His feet were bare, and the carpet beside them was damp, because I'd cleaned it but done a poor job of getting it dry. 'Here he is,' I said, as if he were something to display; then I sat beside him on the bed.

'You're feeling very poorly, aren't you, Mr Perry?' she said, and it struck me then, as it often had before, that 'poorly' was a word parents use for their children, and doctors use only for the very sick. David replied in his quiet hesitant way that yes, he wasn't feeling right – that he kept getting in a muddle; but when he spoke he seemed not to be looking at her, but at me.

'Well,' she said. 'Don't worry. We're going to get things

sorted. Now' – she waved the urine-yellow folder – 'have you filled in your ReSPECT form yet, Mr Perry?' David and I both looked at her in bewilderment, and with the sense that already we'd failed a test.

'I don't know what that is,' I said. 'We haven't been given anything.'

'Oh, *really*,' she said. She was exasperated; and if it was not precisely directed at us, it struck us all the same because we were in the way. 'Really,' she said, 'they really should have sorted this out.' She took a sheet of paper from the folder, which she put beside the books and the Bible on the chest of drawers. 'Now,' she said, 'this is a ReSPECT form. This is about your wishes, Mr Perry.' Again David looked at me, as if the doctor were speaking a dialect he could almost but not quite grasp. I shifted my body nearer his, not for his comfort but for mine: a curious, fearful atmosphere had come with the doctor into the room, like the chill that sometimes rises from a coat when a man has come in from the cold. It was not the fear of death, but of some impassive mechanism that all along had been grinding away in unmarked rooms down hospital corridors, and which really had nothing to do with David's hand in mine, or the loss already opening out in Robert as he drove home down the Acle Straight.

The doctor waved the sheet of paper at us importantly, and though I never had time to look closely at it on that day, or on any of the seven days that followed, I have it here with me now. I find it a pleasant shade of mauve, with the printing a little offset so that some inscrutable black text slips off the margins. On the top left-hand side the word ReSPECT is written in a purple chosen to complement the mauve. The typeface resembles the typeface for a sign on the entrance to a children's playground; the 'e', in lower case, is set within a heart. Underneath this, in a readily legible sans serif font, the title reads *Recommended Summary Plan for Emergency Care and Treatment*, and it amuses me now to think of some committee of physicians, all of them in excellent health, straining to think of a phrase that would fit, more or less, the acronym ReSPECT. What follows is a small box, in that same darker purple, and on it are printed the words *Microsoft Word version 3.5*, with 'version' conspicuously not capitalised. And though it is difficult for me to look at this form without experiencing an echo of that afternoon's bewildered shock, it is also difficult not to find it funny, or to wonder if – two years having passed – dying men and women now are handed version 3.6, with the print margins properly aligned.

The GP took out her pen. 'Now,' she said, 'we need to fill this in. It should have been done by now.' She frowned at the form, which first requires patient and doctor to share an understanding of the patient's condition – '*Metastatic oesophageal cancer*,' she read aloud and without emphasis. David took this blankly in, then looked at me as if I'd manipulated the endoscopic camera, scrutinised images and blood, and diagnosed his condition myself; then 'Yes,' he said, I suppose having seen assent in my face. 'That's right. Yes.'

'Now: does someone have Power of Attorney? That

is in case it is difficult for you to decide how you will be treated.' Silence then, as if David were failing an exam; so 'Yes,' I said, 'that was all sorted a long time ago. Robert – my husband, he'll be here soon – he has Power of Attorney.'

'Good.' She made a note – I relaxed a little. Perhaps we weren't doing so badly, after all.

'Now, David.' She peered at the form. I worried there wasn't enough light to see by. 'Now: what matters most to you? Living as long as possible, or quality of life and comfort?' We might have been students who'd tested her patience with our poor grasp of fact, our failure to prepare. She looked up from the sheet of paper and scrutinised David with her eyebrows raised. There was silence. We waited: she did not fill it. David looked at me again, and I saw then an expression which was new to him, and which became familiar in the days that followed – a baffled and open plea for help, because it was beyond him to grasp what this woman was saying. And though it was beyond me too, I felt myself to have become the mediator between this man losing his foothold on the earth, and this exasperated woman administering the nature and perhaps duration of his death. I had his hand in mine. He went on looking searchingly at me. 'Dad,' I said, 'when the time comes, would you like them to make sure you live as long as you possibly can, even if that might be uncomfortable and difficult? Or do you think it would be better if we did everything we could to make you comfortable and safe?' I did not say: even if this shortens your life.

'Oh no,' he said, not looking at the doctor but at me, for all the world as if I had any power, for all the world as if I weren't as bewildered and frightened as he – 'no,' he said, 'I don't want to be messed about with.'

'Right, good!' said the GP brightly. She made two swift marks on the paper: evidently something was being crossed out. 'And where do you want to be, David?' She did not look at him as she asked, because she was busy signing her name – I can see it now: a brief cipher in cheap black pen – in the box which reads: *Prioritise Comfort*.

'Mr Perry' – evidently we were testing her – 'would you like to be kept here?' There again was David's slow befuddled look, first at the doctor and the paper she held, and then at me. What a terrible responsibility this is, I thought, what a task, to be the interpreter – I found myself speaking to him more gently than I ever had before, all the while wondering if in fact I ought to have been firmer, more precise: 'You know some people go into a hospice, towards the end,' I said, holding David's dismayed gaze, 'or they're taken to hospital, and that's where they die. But some people prefer to remain at home – and we can do that, we can do whatever you ask, but I think she needs us to decide now.' Meanwhile my ordinary unwise self – the woman who had not plummeted that morning down a hatch set in the bedroom wall – looked on as silent and astonished as the painted parrots.

David frowned at me then, as if the question was absurd (I suppose it was): 'No,' he said. 'No, I want to stay here, I want to stay at home.'

'He'd like to stay here,' I said.

'Excellent' – another mark was entered on the page – 'now then.' She lowered the paper and surveyed us both. 'Now then, Mr Perry. What should we do if you become very unwell?' (But he is already very unwell, I thought, and it's only going to get worse.) 'Say we were to come in and something had happened. Say we found you fallen out of bed, over there' – she gestured to the gap between the bed where we sat, and the new curtains we'd only recently admired; and stupidly it occurred to me to point out that the gap was far too narrow, he was surely unlikely to fall in that direction. 'Say we call the ambulance. The paramedics have a choice, don't they? You can be rushed to the Norfolk and Norwich – blue lights, and so on – or they can keep you comfortable here.' She stopped speaking: she'd said her piece, and was bland and untroubled as table staff taking an order. Then again, her impatient silence – again David looking at me, unable to comprehend the absolute absurdity of finding himself barefoot in his own bedroom, asked by a harried stranger to determine the manner and location of his death. 'I think what she means,' I said – I remember how I leaned against him then, pressing my shoulder against his – 'she's talking about resuscitation, Dad – about CPR.' The responsibility I felt then was appalling, because I understood the power and persuasion of language, and it was not for me to tell a man how tight his grasp should be on his own life – 'And of course they can do that, and they will – though they do say it can be rough, you know, quite brutal, what they do to start a heart again, and it doesn't always work – and they'd have to take you away from here. But you must decide – you must tell us what you would like.'

And 'No,' said David, seeming then to arrive at a sudden clarity, 'no, no' – he was speaking to me, and not to her – 'no, I won't be messed about with!'

'Right, good!' said the GP, pleased with herself and with us all. 'Right, so that's DNR!' she said (I heard the exclamation mark). Efficiently she slashed through the parts of the form requesting a return to life – that was now out of the question – and signed the document for the final time. This second signature is less precise than the first – a loop and lift of the pen, small and significant as a rune. It is confined with a box which reads *CPR attempts* **NOT** *recommended*. The box is bordered in red; the word 'not' is capitalised and printed in bold. So between us – hurried, frightened, and anxious to please – we agreed that David's heart when it stopped should be left stopped, that his breath when it gave out should not be returned to him, and that all this should happen there in the bungalow where each evening he made himself porridge for supper. And in the years that have followed, as I've looked over what was said and done in those long peculiar days, and going over my duties have wondered if I carried them out as I ought to have done, I've often been afraid that I influenced him in some way with my mediation.

'So that's that then,' said the doctor, visibly more cheerful now her task was done. She returned the form to the urinous folder and waved it at us: 'Now, this needs to be put somewhere it can be seen. The windowsill, that might be a good place, they'd spot it there, I expect.' Then she handed it to me; but I never did put it on the windowsill, or even look at it in the following days, because already my bewilderment was giving in to anger, and a childish refusal to do as I was told, for all the world as if my rebellion against this woman was rebellion against death.

But she began to speak kindly to David then, I think because she'd begun to grasp the speed of his decline – that he did not consider himself some troublesome invalid for whom life had become tedious, but that less than two months had passed since he'd sat laughing in the Yarmouth Hippodrome until his happiness shook the chair he sat in. 'Things will start to happen soon,' she said – so in fact she was capable of reassurance – 'somebody will be with you tomorrow, and they'll make an assessment of David, and what he needs.'

'Thank you,' I said, with numbed politeness, showing her to the door and watching her go quickly past the lavender bushes and the artificial lawn. She searched for her car keys in her pocket, and when she'd found them she said to me over her shoulder: 'Well, I must be getting on. I'm going on holiday tomorrow, and do you know: I haven't even packed?'

'Oh,' I said, 'I hope you have a lovely time' – then *stupid callous cruel woman*, I thought, closing the door, *what a terrible woman, what a terrible thing*. I thought that often in the weeks that followed, and sometimes think it now – then, like the competing mechanisms of a mechanical clock, there comes a kind of counterbalance: it was not her job to wring her hands, or to eke out our shock – it was her job to see her patient's wishes identified, notified, and carried out. How could she live, if she absorbed the sorrow and dismay of every family told they must prop that yellow folder on the windowsill where it can be seen? And it occurs to me now that perhaps she was really calloused, as I've so often said, since a callus will form in soft places that have too often been rubbed sore.

When I went into the bedroom again, I found David returned to that childlike position into which he always settled himself in those days, and was drowsing. So I left him there, and carried my anger distractedly about the bungalow, waiting for Robert to come. After a time I sat in the little living room, leaving off the lights: it was still possible to make out the winter almond flowering across the lawn, the red geraniums in their pots, the worn place on his tapestry chair. Soon that room would alter, accruing ugly unfamiliar objects littered about the place as if cancer were an animal that had gone through the bungalow leaving behind its spoor. I saw the last of it then as a living room, and not a dying room – the brick hearth displaying an ornamental candle too good to ever be burned, and the brass standard lamp on which a milky glass globe was supported by metal leaves peeling, over the years, further and further back from the light; the immense needlepoint of flowers done by Robert's great-aunt Ruth, who'd done remarkable things in the war for the St John Ambulance, and the heavy coffee table with its inlaid tiles scattered with puzzle books, stamps, unopened post, a basket of pegs he'd taken from the cupboard because he'd been intending to hang the washing out. In the corner there was a large cabinet in dark varnished wood with glass doors, and here David kept things he thought too good to be used or handled, or even seen too often – what remained of his florid wedding china with fluted rims, and a cactus my grandmother made in green smocked silk, which for twenty years had passed for the real thing until the green silk faded; a silver paperknife, and a badly done watercolour of a hibiscus I'd painted for Jenny when I was seventeen, and her hip had been replaced. Set back on a glass shelf there was a small photo in a plain frame. David and Jenny rarely took family photos, or displayed them: they were never sentimental people. This I think was because when Jenny was a child of eight, her mother had died in childbirth, leaving two daughters behind. Her mother had been a redhead, and sometimes Robert has said what a shame it is that there are no colour photos of her, since he'd have liked to have seen for himself his lost grandmother's blaze of hair (and in the brief time we wanted children, we'd often said how nice it would be if that red-headed gene came out of recession, and we had a daughter with auburn hair, and perhaps the spirit to match it). So Jenny and her sister had been raised by a father whose own hair had gone quickly white with shock, and by their aunt, who made beautiful clothing and whom they considered their mother. This early loss had given Jenny a mistrust of holding on to what was past, or even pausing to glance over her shoulder and look back down the road – 'Oh just get rid of it,' she'd cheerfully say, 'we don't need that old thing.' But this small photo had been preserved, and I can see it now on our mantelpiece, propped beside a pot of hyacinths that got forced by the heat of the fire and went over too early. The frame is of heavy silver, and I can never keep up with the tarnish; six hallmarks are imprinted on the lower part, and of these I can make out a Tudor rose, a lion rampant, and what appears to be an image of a Concorde aeroplane. The photo is of the kind taken in a photobooth, and I imagine Jenny had been sitting on David's lap, on one of those stools that swivel to allow the subject to position themselves in front of the camera. It must have been winter then. Jenny wears a coat in pale wool with a brooch pinned to the collar. David has on a tie and dark jacket; his hair is black and neatly brushed, and he is looking into the distance beyond the lens. Jenny is smiling, but her gaze is direct, astute: she seems now to be assessing me, to be saying 'What do you want to go over all that for, my girl? Just get rid of it, you don't need that old thing.'

Her hair in this photo is short, straight, and almost chic. I only ever knew it curled by frequent perms, and was often tasked with combing it for her because by then she was unable to raise her arms, and she said I did it more gently than David (and I remember now that sometimes I did this with bad grace, though I can't imagine why, or excuse having ever been such a selfish heartless child). Already in that photobooth she'd been sick with rheumatoid arthritis for years, and her hands were traced with surgical scars. Once, as she'd travelled with David on a train, her skirt had ridden above her knees, and he'd told her that she had only let that happen because she knew perfectly well that her scars were sexy – she told me this with confiding mischief when both David and Robert were out of the room, and it had been so out of keeping with a woman who seemed to me already very old by then, whom I'd first met in the chapel pews, that I was mortified and changed the subject. And because of her illness, it was thought unlikely she'd be able to conceive or carry a child, so that when Robert was born he was a celebrated baby, passed around the church and the library and wherever she took him; and he was such a beautiful baby, she said, everyone told her she ought to enter him into competitions – but that was unthinkable, since she'd be so angry if he didn't win that it wasn't worth the bother.

Surveying the photo in the cabinet, hearing David turning sometimes in the room next door, I thought how rarely he spoke of her, and how in a man of his nature silence on a subject can indicate depth of feeling, not lack of it. 'If I loved you less,' said Mr Knightley in Jane Austen's *Emma*, 'I might be able to talk about it more.' His faith, I knew, was more fixed and sincere than mine had ever been, and in the past weeks he'd mentioned God as rarely as he ever mentioned Jenny, and I wonder now whether if he believed less, he might have talked about it more. I wanted then – I want now – to believe what I suppose he believed: that before long, and sooner than he'd thought, he'd be crossing over the River Jordan – that there'd be peace in the valley where the lion lay down with the lamb, and that Jenny would be waiting for him there. And since it must be in the nature of heaven to feel no loss or sorrow, I suppose David thought that the ten years he had spent without Jenny had been no time at all for her, so that in fact she'd felt no sorrow at missing her husband – and that since in heaven there can be no sickness or injury, he'd never again admire the scars he'd loved.

It is not possible to see, in this photo, the colour of Jenny's cheeks, which were always covered with a fine tracery of broken blood vessels, and gave the impression from a distance that she was wearing blusher, or in very good health. I only once saw her cheeks pale, and that was when we sat with her after she'd died alone on a hospital ward and (this is the story we tell each other) in her sleep. David had called with the news in the early hours. We were living in London then, and though I passed the phone to Robert I knew from the deadened tone of David's voice what news he was giving to his son – 'She's gone,' I faintly heard him say, 'she's gone.' So we took the earliest of that day's trains to Essex, and went on to the Basildon hospital where her organs had been failing from sepsis, and where the previous day she'd sent us all home with those kisses hurled across the room and twenty pounds for the cab. The nurse who greeted us on the ward left us for a long while beside the bed with Jenny in it, all of us enclosed by papery blue curtains, and so little going on elsewhere there was the impression that every other patient had been cured and sent home. Robert remembers how often this same nurse had said to him, 'She is dead. She is dead,' all the while handing out forms to fill in and a plastic pen to fill them with, and that he felt this was because in her experience the fact of a death is so unlikely, and so absurd, that family members must have it repeated baldly before they can take it in. I remember David holding her hand – I remember Robert stooping to kiss her cheek. I did neither: a kind of intense interest had taken me over, and I examined the cheeks which had lost their colour, and the rim of moisture blotting the pillow in a dark halo around the curls she'd never been able to brush herself. Later, on the train home, Robert had looked dazedly out of the window and said, 'Well: these things do happen. These things do happen, don't they?', because it was a long time before he understood the scale and permanence of the loss. Then – abruptly less dazed, and more astute – he'd looked at me and said: 'You're going to write about this, aren't you?'

'Yes,' I said, without apology or explanation. 'Yes, I will.'

'Good,' he'd said, returning to the window. The sun was high by then. 'You should.'

And on that evening after the doctor left us, as I sat nursing my bewildered anger and waiting for Robert to come, I understood that already I'd begun to form images and paragraphs out of what was happening to David; that I watched him not only with love's frightened attention, but with the assessing acquisitive eye of a magpie. The French rabbi Delphine Horvilleur, in her book *Living with Our Dead*, writes of the sacred stories connecting the living with the dead: 'The role of the storyteller,' she says, 'is to stand by the gate to ensure it stays open.' I can't say it was sacred of me to sit in that dark room and wonder how, in time, I'd convey what was happening, and what I knew would happen soon. But I do think that evening I took up my post by an opening gate and have stood there ever since. What else am I supposed to do?

When Robert came home later that evening down the Acle Straight, having explained with embarrassment to his new colleagues that he was unable for the moment to return to his work, I turned on all the lights to greet him, and thought how immense his body seemed to me then, how indestructible, as if the solidity of his presence tipped back the balance and might keep us all from falling. I'd been lonely and afraid, and was never more glad to see him; but I understood even then that the loss in store for me was insignificant compared to what was waiting for him. He had a black bin bag with him. He'd gone home and filled this bag with clothes for himself, and with a quilt he'd taken from our bed together with a single pillow. So we made a nest on the floor of the room where David managed his immense collection of stamps, and passed hours sorting those he'd keep from ones he'd trade, listening to cricket or early rock 'n' roll on the radio. I'd never paid much attention to David's stamps, and so it was not until that evening, as we set aside that part of his life, I realised how devoted he'd been to this hobby – scattered where he'd left them on the pale pine desk he'd bought for the purpose were long-tipped forceps for lifting the frailest stamps without tearing the serrated edge, magnifying glasses for examining what remained of franking marks, and a lamp with a blue-tinged bulb designed to mimic daylight after the sun had gone down. More than once he'd told me that among the most valuable stamps in the world were a handful that had been issued in South Africa, and were smeared with blood because a postman had been killed by a lion as he did his rounds, and dropped the contents of his sack in the struggle. At least: that is how I remember the story, and since I'd rather believe it than not I've never thought to prove or disprove it. And as we pushed aside the boxes of stamps and the wheeled chair where David had so often sat, and tried to make a comfortable place for Robert to sleep, I told him about the GP, and the form in its yellow plastic folder which I'd left somewhere in the bedroom where it could be found by paramedics if they came – if, for example, David fell improbably down between the bed and the wall. It was difficult not to say aloud what I had been thinking all afternoon – what a terrible callous woman she'd been! What a cold and hectoring manner! – because that would have done nothing but hand the anger on, and Robert already had more to bear than I did. But listening quietly he said that his father had done exactly as he'd imagined he would – that of course he'd want to be here at home, and not alone on a ward as Jenny had been, under some flickering strip-light down some corridor with a faded linoleum floor, signs above the door in the lifeless NHS blue, papery blue curtains pulled back and forth too early in the morning and too late at night, disposable blue aprons whispering over the uniforms of nurses coming to draw blood – and of course he wouldn't want to be messed about with, that was exactly the sort of thing he would say. I felt childishly that I'd done well, and been told I'd done well, then was afraid that I had done what I'd done for the sake of praise.

Soon after this, as David was sleeping, someone came to collect me and take me home to the dogs, and I walked into a hiatus. It seemed odd to me and even offensive that nothing had altered in my absence – half-read books were put where I'd left them, their spines cracked and pages folded because I've never taken care of my books, not since I was a child; bottles of perfume with the caps left off; bread not yet gone stale in the kitchen (though if I'd gone into my study I might have found the coffee-stained envelope on which I'd calculated the daily calories David needed to keep himself alive). For an hour or so I tried my hand at what I might have been doing, if David had not begun to die – emails were going unanswered, laundry was going unwashed – but all the time there was the nauseated sensation of having been arrested only briefly during a long fall. In the end, and uncertain of sleep, I phoned my eldest sister, who for some years had been an end-of-life carer: a kind of midwife, as I'd always thought of it, for the second and final labour. I said to her then what I'd been saying for weeks – that he was dying, and doing it quickly, that he couldn't possibly be left alone. 'Can he breathe without help?' she said. She has always been softly spoken, and though her voice was soft then it was so altered by authority I might not have known it was her, without the evidence of her name on the phone's screen.

'Oh yes, yes, he can. His breathing is the same as it always was.'

'Is he in any pain?'

'We ask and ask, and he says no.'

'Does he eat and drink?'

'He has ice cream sometimes, and squash.'

'Has he asked you never to leave him?'

'No, but I don't think he ever would, not even –'

'He's all right for now, Sarah. Try not to worry. And get some sleep.'

I tried not to worry. I did sleep.

~

It is the night of November 15th, 2022. It is one day since David was given his diagnosis; it is eight days until he will die. It is quiet in Norwich, which is a quiet city, and the bungalow is in a quiet suburb. David is sleeping curled like a child on his side. The red numbers on the alarm-clock radio tick silently over: now it is the morning of November 16th, and seven days until he will die. When the sun comes up it will appear there are more and more flowers on the almond tree, but the geraniums are on their way out. Only so much bloom to go round. Robert is sometimes sleeping on the floor of the room across the hall, under the patchwork quilt my grandmother made for our wedding gift, and which contains scraps of the dresses I wore as a child. He is woken now and then by incoherent cries that come from his father's room; when he goes to look, to see that David is safe at least, he finds him peaceably sleeping. The following morning he'll tell me that his father has always done this – that even when Robert was a boy he'd hear a wordless muffled yell from his parents' room across the landing at the head of the stairs, and that David in the morning would know nothing about it, and not even remember his dreams. Once, when he's woken too thoroughly and can't sleep again, Robert goes to make himself a drink, to find something to eat. He's often stood there in his father's kitchen, opening drawers to find a teaspoon to stir sweeteners into a mug of tea, but in the secretive small-hours lamplight he sees something that had for some reason passed him by – a fork made of a light metal alloy, the handle a bulky tube of pale plastic. This had been Jenny's fork, designed to be grasped with hands that towards the end of her life resembled the satiny paws of a furless animal. Robert remembered then that in the days after she'd died we'd go to the house in Basildon and find her possessions scattered in various bins – her hair comb, hand cream, a pair of gloves – because she and David had not been sentimental people and 'Just get rid of it,' she would have said, 'you don't need those old things.' But David has kept this old thing, perhaps thinking it might come in useful or perhaps out of sentiment; and Robert, not able to look at it for long, closes the drawer quickly and goes back to his mattress on the floor.

When David woke later that same morning he discovered he no longer lived alone. The faded floral quilt was curiously weighted and this made it difficult to move; the curtains were open to reveal the thin veil which the seamstress who made them had insisted he call 'voiles', and not 'nets' – he'd found it funny then, and often said 'voiles' to himself when he stood at the window; he found it funny now. Out in the kitchen somebody was on the phone. When eventually he raised himself on his elbows he was surprised to find our dogs lying immobile at his feet – 'Hello, Ruby,' he said, 'hello, Janey,' accepting their presence, reaching for Janey in his distracted affectionate way, for the fawn-coloured ears that curled back from her cautiously tragic black eyes; and possibly thinking, as I often thought in those days, how they were like the marble hounds sleeping at the feet of the lovers holding hands on the Arundel Tomb. It was all right, he thought, to lie there for a time, there was nothing he could think of that he ought to be doing; though he could pick out, in the first light sifting in, things in his bedroom that he'd never seen before. He was thirsty, and wondered what he wanted to drink. His hearing was then, and remained almost until the end, remarkably acute, and after a time he understood who it was that was speaking on the phone, and that the tone was anxious and even argumentative, so that when I'd finished the call and came in he was expecting me, and had begun to worry that he was being a bother. 'OK,' he said, 'everything OK?' and yes, I said – it's just that we could do with some help, but it was all right: they were sending someone soon.

'I'm being a bother,' he said, but it was not the tone of the previous day, when he seemed to regret the bother and even to be irritated with himself for needing help, and irritated with us for needing to give it. Already he was becoming resigned, and this made it possible for me to smile and say, 'An awful bother actually, yes, awful!' I sat on the bed. I wondered if I ought to take his hand, and in my wondering I left it too late, and was unable to do it. Robert, hearing us speak, came in, and I saw for the first time that he'd developed a new way of looking at his father, which was something like shyness, as if he were being introduced to somebody new whom for some reason he felt he'd like to please. 'Morning, Dad,' he said, 'how did you sleep?'

'Yes, very well thank you,' said David. 'Very well, yes.'

'We've moved in,' I said. 'Do you mind the dogs?' – but I could see he didn't mind them, though Ruby by then was standing over him, turning and turning in some mysterious discomfort before settling again in the same pose and in the same place. 'Do you want a cup of tea?' I said, all the while recalling my sister's soft and altered voice, and assessing his capacity – was his breathing as it had always been? Did he show signs of pain? It was, and he didn't – but overnight, I thought, something had happened to his hands, which now were mottled all over with age-spots, the knuckles swollen as if he'd been fighting.

'Squash,' he said. He was decisive: 'I'd like some squash. But I need the toilet.'

'Right!' I said (and I spoke too brightly). 'Look, we

got this, from Argos. It's funny, they sell everything there, don't they?' Robert brought forward the walking frame he'd collected that morning, at the hour the shop by the river had opened. David looked at it – 'Right,' he said, 'yes, good, excellent,' and did not, as I'd feared, seem to resent this material evidence of his decline, which I'd expected and would have forgiven. Slowly he moved himself to the edge of the bed and set his bare feet on the carpet, and I saw that in my absence Robert had helped his father change out of the clothes he'd worn to the hospital and into cotton pyjamas printed all over with blue hibiscus flowers. David had chosen these himself – he must have done: there was nobody else who would do it – and they so diminished his look of sickness and dependence that I felt my spirits lift. He'd used a walking frame before, when his hip had been replaced, so it gave him no bother, and I recall the relief I felt then that he could at least take himself across the hall to the bathroom – we were falling, it was true, but there was no acceleration, as the laws of physics demanded: we did not for example need to take an arm each and coax a failing body on to a toilet seat. So it was difficult not to say, 'Well done!', as if praising a child; but Robert and I watched him and watched each other with gratitude and possibly self-congratulation – there, hadn't we all done well. We were coping, we felt, the three of us, and the damp place on the carpet had dried.

'Someone is coming to help us,' I had told David; and very soon somebody did. She came so early that day, and was the first of so many, that we've said to each other often that as much as the GP had frightened us, she must have frightened others, and this thought always makes my anger recede for a time. This woman introduced herself, and explained that she was from the community nursing team: David was now under their care. She had a face which I persuaded myself was very like my sister's face – soft, good-natured and pretty; falling naturally into a melancholy expression whenever she wasn't speaking – and a gentle authoritative voice that was also like hers. She handed David a leaflet printed on flimsy paper with a grainy feel, and which I think had been designed to be consoling; but its illustrations had come out too dark, so that in the photos on the front page it was difficult to distinguish the patients from the nurses, and in an image of a hand in a wrinkled and blue disposable glove it was clear that someone was doing something to somebody, but it was impossible to say what. The leaflet had a logo of a butterfly made up of many small red objects: the butterfly's thorax was composed of a stethoscope and a syringe; the wings contained an ambulance, a crab, and a pulled tooth. The woman sat on the bed between the dogs and asked the questions my sister had asked: was he breathing all right? He was, and that was good. And was he in pain? He said he was not in pain.

'What about toileting?' she said, and we told her that toileting was all right, really, now that we had a walking frame and he could get to the bathroom in time. 'But it's been a long time since he had a bowel movement,' I said, finding myself rather prurient and foolish.

'Days, actually, yes,' said David; and the nurse looked at us then with an expression that became briefly more acute. She made a note. When with some pride we showed her the Argos walking frame, she said that no, no, that would never do – look, it wasn't secure or safe, and a better one would come later that same day. 'And I'll get you a raised toilet seat,' she said, making a note, 'he'll find that helpful, and a commode.' She looked up from her papers and said with some additional delicacy: 'That is for if the time comes when David is perhaps not able to make it to the bathroom.' All the while David was composed and occasionally humorous, answering for himself and seeming to bear no resemblance to the man who'd been mute with shocked exhaustion as the consultant came to take his chair. Robert and I – keeping to the margins of the room, wanting David to speak for himself – sometimes interjected: yes, it's true he was eating, though not very much; should we carry on with the Complan? Very well, then, we would.

'And they're fitting a stent,' said Robert, 'in three days' time, and that will make a difference.'

'All the difference in the world,' I said. 'He'll be able to eat again, that's what they say.'

This delighted the woman. 'Ah,' she said, 'that can be transformative. There, David: you will have to think of all the things you'll be able to enjoy again. Now,' she said, 'we can look into arranging carers when the time comes –'

'Oh, yes: thank you, thank you,' I said. Then it struck me that I'd seemed too hasty then, and too relieved; that

I'd betrayed how unsuited I was to all this. I said, 'We've moved in, you see. So I'm sure we'll be all right, for now.' Now she was smiling, and I felt that her smile took us all in – that David was being a good invalid, and Robert was being a good son – felt, in fact, that I understood each of us in that room, and that David was thinking: well, this is sooner than I expected, though seventy-seven isn't a bad innings, not really. But I'm being a bit of a bother and they do look tired don't they, should get themselves some lunch. Yes, much sooner, all happening fast, it won't be long, Jenny, not too long now – and this woman, nurse did she say? – she's excellent isn't she, really excellent – I can't need the toilet again, not already. Something going on in my back, isn't there, something not right – might mention it, but don't want to be more of a bother –

The woman was thinking: nice man isn't he, nice family, not doing too badly, doesn't need a wheelchair yet, doesn't need any help to eat or drink for example, no pain or difficulty breathing – should air this room out a bit, though. Sweet dogs these, what are they, whippet is it, this one, looks more like a deer than a dog, eyes a bit foggy, might be going blind – next appointment in ten minutes, never really enough time is there but traffic won't be too bad by now, school drop-off was a while back, don't forget to leave a copy of the file –

Robert was thinking: my father is dying? My father is going to die?

I was thinking: that's novelists all over, isn't it, think we can read minds because we're so used to writing them, think we can control the weather. I do wish I could go home.

When the woman got up from the bed she grasped David's foot through the quilt and released it quickly. 'Thank you, David,' she said. 'Thank you for your time. We've got it all in hand. Things will come today and tomorrow: we'll look after you.' Then she handed me a leaflet of half A4 size in that same soft and grainy paper. 'Keep this with you' – her voice, if gentle, becoming more authoritative – 'you'll need it.'

I have it here with me now, and it surprises me to find I'm able these days to look at it directly, because there was a time the sight of it caused a shock of chilled nausea I couldn't control, and in fact days after the death I'd see it printed on my vision, in the way a blot of light will stain the whole view if you look too long at the sun. WHO TO CALL? it reads, in red capital letters; underneath this there is a red picture of an old-fashioned rotary phone, the receiver on a coiled wire levitating above the cradle with the caller's desperation. There follows a list of numbers which, called at any time of the day or night, would summon somebody from the 'community hub'. And though it was never clear to me either then or now what authority was responsible for this hub, or who it was that would take the call, I came to depend on this piece of paper as if I were a failed saint and it had been an icon in a gilded frame. It has been folded and unfolded too many times, and is on the verge of splitting; my handwriting is all over it – *re syringe driver ready to pick up* and *ask DN re barrier cream or spray* and *NIGHT* underlined twice. In places I have written words and phrases, then fiercely scribbled them out, and I can't see or remember what I was thinking at the time. But when I took it from her that afternoon it was unmarked and unremarkable – I thanked her; then I put it somewhere too safe, so that when I did need it, and sooner than she'd thought, I couldn't find it for a while.

When the woman left us, it seemed to me that the atmosphere in the bungalow had altered. The panic I'd experienced the previous day, and which had been the proof and fulfilment of our weeks of dread since we'd seen death coming over the market square, receded. It was true that we'd fallen down a hatch, but we were falling together, and as it turned out there were people waiting down there with their forms, their community hub and their commodes. David, propped on pillows among the parrots, never seemed confused or even especially troubled, though it frustrated him to find that he needed to urinate frequently and in quantities that were out of keeping with the sips of tea and orange squash he took; so back and forth he went, the walking frame thudding decisively on the carpet, the toilet cistern noisily filling. Robert seemed able to look at his father again, and wandered in and out of the bedroom talking about the news, or handing him opened post. A friend came, greeted David as briefly and easily as if it had been a social occasion, cleaned the kitchen which still had spilled oats on the floor and countertop, and left us with a bag of pastries. Towards the end of the afternoon a van drew up, and cheerful efficient men in monogrammed polo shirts brought the officially sanctioned walking frame, and a commode resembling an ordinary office chair with an artificial-leather seat that could be lifted to reveal a white plastic container. Together we looked at this object with dislike and disbelief: it was a thing that belonged in a nursing home or a hospital ward, and surely it would never be needed – so we pushed it to the furthest corner of David's room, and this act represented the curious suspended state in which we found ourselves: halfway between our half-prophetic certainty that David was dying, and doing it quickly, and a refusal to countenance anything so absurd.

Luther came back to the bungalow that day, shortly after the cheerful efficient men had gone away in their van. It was difficult to know how to greet him – he was David's pastor and not mine; and besides, it had been years since my faith had kept me in the pews. He wore his ordinary clothes, since Baptist ministers will show their calling in their demeanour and not their collar; he had a Bible under his arm. When he came in, I suppose he brought God with him. But what he also brought – as substantially as if I'd been able to see it behind him when I went to open the door – was the life which had been familiar to David, which he'd shared with Jenny and with his son and would never take part in again: the hymns he always sang badly, having a tin ear for the tune; the chapel teas; the conversations in the car park when the services were over and the weather was good. So I was glad to take Luther into the bedroom and leave him there, while I made myself busy in the kitchen and overheard him speaking and praying with his tentative authority. And at this time it struck me that I hadn't prayed for David, or for any of us, since this had all begun – had never gone to my knees and cried *Make haste O God to deliver me, make haste to help me O Lord* – and that this wasn't because I felt God wouldn't trouble himself to intervene, but because it hadn't occurred to me. In fact I only prayed once during that time, and this was towards the end; and not with words, but with the movement of my arms.

That night, lying with Robert and the dogs on the mattress on the floor, I felt again that we'd been arrested during a fall, with no more shocks, no troubling changes. Perhaps after all it would be a long and slow decline – the nurse when she visited had not seemed especially troubled; perhaps we would after all have time to be ground down, and that would be a relief. When, in the middle of the night, I heard David begin to cry out, I crossed the hall to see him, and by the light of my phone found him sleeping toppled on his left side, safely confined by the floral quilt, the commode and the walking frame where we'd left them, the parrots awake on the wall. I listened, and he cried out again; but it was wordless, and seemed to have no more meaning or significance than if he'd begun to snore. So I left him, went back to our mattress, and slept.

The Palazzo Cartelloni in Florence, a city I've never seen, was owned once by the mathematician Vincenzo Viviani, who was the student and biographer of Galileo Galilei (and for whom the Viviani lunar crater is named, which none of us have ever seen, because it's on the other side of the moon). Above the palazzo door there is a marble bust of Galileo, who to my eye resembles Nicholas, the last Tsar of Russia, who at the age of fifty was shot by Bolsheviks in a basement room, together with his family. Flanking the door and the bust there are two vast stone scrolls, on which Viviani had engraved in Latin a life of Galileo and a celebration of his accomplishments, such as his observations of the rings of Saturn and the moons of Jupiter. Though Galileo is most commonly associated with the movement of the earth around the sun, he also looked downwards, and considered the nature of gravity and the way things fall, and once devised an experiment in which, as he wrote in his *Dialogues on Motion*, 'In a plank of wood . . . we made upon the narrow side a groove . . . and to make it very smooth and sleek, we glued upon it a piece of vellum, and in that we let fall a very hard, round, and smooth brass ball.' Again and again this brass ball was made to roll down the plank of wood, which was kept at an incline, and by measuring the time it took the ball to roll down different lengths of the plank, Galileo was able to prove that all falling objects will accelerate, until enough resistance is met to cause the limit of their speed (Galileo died, by the way, at the age of seventy-seven, which is the age that David died; and he too died in his own home, if under house arrest. He was by then half-blind and bad-tempered, with a hernia and heart palpitations and no appetite for food; but all the same he retained to the end his essential Galileo-ness, complaining to his friends, 'I cannot keep my restless brain from grinding on, although with great loss of time . . .'). Though the custom in those days was for natural philosophers to write in Latin, Galileo wrote in Italian because, as he said, he wanted everyone to read what he wrote, and to know that 'just as Nature has given eyes to them for the purpose of seeing her works, she has also given them brains for examining and understanding them.'

I should have been Galileo's pupil: I should have remembered the way things fall. I was still at that time preoccupied with the novel I'd just written, in which the laws of physics are taken as parables for the ways we live and move and have our being – so really it should have occurred to me that if we were falling, as I kept saying we were, we could never have been arrested in motion: that all along David had been falling faster and faster, and nothing could be done to stop it – and that this was as natural as an apple at the end of summer dropping from the tree.

I woke early the following morning, disoriented for a moment by my view of David's stamp collection stored in its translucent white boxes, and his handsome set of Folio Society hardbacks that served that week as the headboard of our bed. Then I understood where I was, and why I was there, and so my heart began its fretful beat – *little pig, little pig, let me come in*. Robert was still sleeping, and since sleep had eased the strain on his face he looked no older than he'd been when we were first married, in the days when it still shocked me to find another pillow by my pillow and another head by my head, and I'd wake early and look at him and think: I am only twenty, and this is my life, and I am in it. I stood quietly. I thought: now this is our life, and we are in it. I left Robert sleeping. It was silent in the bungalow; the sun was only halfway up, and there was no traffic yet on the roads. The dogs lifted their heads, looked at me once, and returned to their sleep. David was profligate with the thermostat and the place was very warm. I stood in the hallway in my nightdress outside David's door, and as I listened I heard movements under the quilt that were fretful and small like the movements of an animal in the undergrowth at night. 'Dad?' I said, speaking softly, hoping I suppose that he'd go on sleeping and I wouldn't yet have to face the day; then I went in. I could make out the red numbers of the alarm-clock radio, and the white seat of the commode (and I knew that somewhere in there, disobediently out of sight, was the urine-yellow folder); the curtains had not quite been properly closed, and I saw the headlights of a neighbour's car setting out on their unremarkable day. I turned on the lamp. 'Dad?' I said. His back was towards me, and he was curled again on his left side, but with a series of slow arduous movements was bringing himself towards the edge of the bed. I could see the soles of his bare feet extending now from beyond the quilt, and I noticed then how soft they were – how the toenails were kept in good order, for all that I could never get him to clean his glasses, or have his false teeth mended. 'Is everything OK,' I said, 'are you in pain?', because that was always what occurred to me first. 'Yes, OK,' he said – he mumbled, as if barely awake – 'just need the toilet'; and there was the impression he'd needed the toilet for some time, but we hadn't thought to leave him a way of summoning our help. Now he was positioned near the edge of the bed, and with his elbow pressed against the mattress was attempting to bring himself upright. So I gave him my arm, and thought again how astonishing it was that even an old man and a sick one could be made of such dense matter; 'Let me try,' I said, 'let me help' – but Robert by then had heard us, and come wearily in. 'Morning,' he said, with his new shy way of not quite looking at his father. Then – expertly, because of the years he'd spent caring for Jenny – he brought David to a standing position and presented him with the walking frame the nurse had left us. For a moment David stood between us grasping the frame as if he stood on the pitching deck of a ship, and needed purchase. He had always been more or less exactly the height of his son, if only he could be persuaded to stand up straight; but I noticed then that he seemed to have become shorter while we slept, and now was no taller than me. Then with a determined motion of his head he said, 'Right!', seeming to have woken finally out of a dragging sleep, and lifting the frame and setting it down with decisive movements he headed for the bathroom. Robert and I looked at each other in relief – there: it wasn't so bad as all that – but then David paused at the threshold and looked down at himself with a puzzled expression. He said nothing for a time, then 'Oh,' he said, 'I've got in a muddle,' and

I saw the blue hibiscus pyjamas were becoming soaked with urine that was pouring out of him as if from an upturned jug.

Often in the weeks that followed I told friends and strangers what happened next, and understood how absurd I sound – but I've gone on telling it, and I'll tell it again: in that first moment after David's incontinence began I felt a woman's hand on my shoulder. I've rarely thought of myself as a woman, and certainly not a very satisfactory one – I failed to want children as much as I ought to have done, for example, and my feminism has always seemed to me a political position, and nothing to do with my female identity, which I have found largely irrelevant. I say to myself that I'd be no less a feminist if I'd been a man, and no less indignant: I've never wanted to dance with the sisterhood; could never, at any rate with a straight face, claim to be a daughter of the witches they couldn't burn. But as I saw David standing there, looking down at himself as if he'd become a problem he couldn't solve, women claimed me, and greatly against my will. It was a physical sensation, and I understood – or seemed to understand – that a woman was standing behind me with her hand on my right shoulder, and that possibly this was my mother, or someone's mother at any rate – and that she, too, felt a hand on her right shoulder, and that this chain went on and on, back through preceding generations of women who'd stood in bungalows like these, or terraced houses, or cottages with plaster falling off the brick, or apartments in new blocks where the plaster was still wet on the walls, and prepared themselves for the death watch. And if I can't tell this story without embarrassment – I find it politically indefensible, and I cannot make it sit with my sense of myself as a creature of reason – I tell it anyway, since I suppose truth is more valuable to me than reputation. Moments before, it would have appalled me to think that I might see David incontinent, or to contemplate the necessity of changing his clothes and washing him, and the affront to his dignity and mine which this would represent. I would have recoiled, I would have retreated to the discarnate safety of my desk, my books, my telescope: all that was the work of the professionals, I'd have said, it ought to be undertaken behind decently closed doors. But that line of women summoned up briefly in the bedroom of a Norwich bungalow had all done what needed to be done, because there was nobody else who could do it, and they assured me that I was going to do it too. What had seemed to me a breach in my unremarkable life now seemed an unremarkable part of it, and as instinctive and natural as helping up a child who'd fallen over. When I spoke to David then, I heard with relief and astonishment that the bright, nannying tone I'd adopted in the preceding days had gone, and that I was speaking as myself again.

'Do you think you've finished?' I said. 'Do you think that's it?'

'Yes,' said David, 'I think so'; and he said again it was just that he'd got in a bit of a muddle.

'Don't worry about it' – I was speaking to myself, and to us all (and behind me the line of women, already and permanently receding, shrugged and said: *See? We told you so*). 'Don't worry. Just wait a moment,' I said, 'let's get a flannel and a towel.' And it was easy then to wash and dry him, and to fetch a clean pair of pyjamas; to say he might as well get back into bed, only we'd have to move Ruby away, she always would take the pillow if she could. Robert brought his father the orange squash he'd asked for, and though we talked for a while – watching covertly to see that David finished his drink, and asking without hope if he wanted a bowl of porridge, or a yogurt – we didn't mention what had happened, and it passed with no more notice than if he'd asked for a tissue when he sneezed.

This is not to say that in the days following I was always competent and cheerful and kind. Over and over I failed to be any of these things, and was often exhausted and resentful and desperately sad. What I mean is that my resentment and sorrow seemed unremarkable, because they were part of my condition in being alive. A few weeks after this I went to a party in London, dressed in an elaborate blue silk coat I'd chosen for myself while David lay dying. I don't often go to parties, and generally dislike them when I do; but had a phase then of accepting every invitation I was offered as if I felt I might die before any others were extended. I met a woman there whose father had recently had a diagnosis that might perhaps prove fatal, and I could see her trying to accommodate this as wine was poured and drunk around us, and assess what it meant for him, and for herself. 'It's going to be all right,' I told her. 'You'll know what to do, I promise: death is just another part of life. You'll think you won't be capable of helping when he becomes incontinent, because he will, you know – that's all a part of it. But I promise: you'll know what to do.' Then I wrapped my coat around me and went out to smoke a Silk Cut, having no idea then, or for a long time after, that I'd developed a habit of being both too intimate and too morbid, as if Banquo's ghost had been at the wine, and gone about embracing every guest at the feast.

I have said it never occurred to me to pray – but it strikes me as I write that in fact I did pray, over and over, if prayer is the act of petitioning unseen powers for help, and trusting it will come. The prayers began that morning, as we returned David to his bed, and having opened the curtains discovered by the honest daylight that he was changing, as if sloughing himself off. His knuckles were swollen, and his hands darker than ever with liver-spots; the swell of his stomach – where three days before he'd rested his mug of tea as he sat cheerfully talking with Janey at his side – was diminishing by the hour, and the face which had always been plump, and which like Robert's was always dimpled when he smiled, had become lean and grave. At certain angles, and in certain lights, I thought I could make out the divots in his skull where his eyes were set. He'd asked for squash, but was disinclined to drink it, and when he did drink he seemed to have difficulty bringing the cup to his mouth. When we offered him porridge or Complan or even the ice cream that was his weakness, he declined with a vague but definite gesture, as if bemused we could have suggested it. Then abruptly a kind of contented exhaustion took him over, so we moved aside the pillows that had been propped against the parrots and brought him down to rest on his back – though I noticed that by the time we'd reached the door, he'd returned once again to the position in which I'd found him that first morning: toppled on to his left-hand side and with his knees drawn up, which I suppose is how he would have rested in the womb.

In the kitchen Robert and I looked at each other for a time and without speaking. There again was that feeling of being caught between our private convictions, and the untroubled assurances of those who'd seen it all before. On the one hand he was falling, and accelerating as all falling objects must; and if you'd asked us we would have said: oh, there are days left, no more than a week – there's death in his swollen knuckles, in the drag of his cheek against his cheekbones, in the urine tang persisting in the hall – didn't we tell you? Didn't we say? Then again that was not possible, surely – men didn't simply die in their own beds days after their cancer was confirmed in language that was evasive because it was kind, and with nothing but a bewildered son and his wife to oversee it. There ought to be appointments, treatments, and mislaid letters from one consultant to another – dreary afternoons in waiting rooms, and medications we were unable to pronounce; visitors coming less and less frequently as the illness dragged on, halting conversations about the choice of funeral hymns, the not unpleasant melancholy of one last Christmas, one final Easter; 'Let's take him to Yarmouth again shall we, love — while the weather's still fine?' — this plummet was indecent, it wasn't the done thing at all. Besides, the woman who'd come to assess him, and had sat with the dogs at the foot of the bed, had surely not seen death at the threshold, or she'd have sent someone to take the matter out of our hands. And there was the stent to think of, which would be fitted in the morning — and that would make all the difference (they said), all the difference in the world.

'I think he is starving,' I said. 'We are watching a man starve to death.'

'Yes,' said Robert, 'that's what it is: it's been days since he ate, and you know I've sometimes wondered if for a long time when he told me he was eating, it really was only porridge or milk.'

'When they put in the stent,' I said, 'we can give him ice cream and mashed potato and so on.' We'd begun to think of the fitting of the stent as if it were a visit to Lourdes and the expectation of a miracle; but already it seemed to me impossible that we could get David to the hospital, and in fact cruel that we should even try. 'Do you think we should tell them?' I said, seeing that Robert was as anxious as I at the prospect of putting the authorities to any further trouble, or of interfering in the operations of the machinery. 'Don't you think we should call?' So I sought out the soft sheet of paper — WHO TO CALL? — and began to ask for help. I was never clear, then or later, who I was speaking to, or who I ought to be speaking to; and before long, as the demarcations between day and night became irrelevant and together with David we entered a state of perpetual dusk, it really did come to feel like prayer – *Make haste O Community Hub to deliver us: make haste to help us, O Hub.* Quickly it became apparent that the speed of David's fall was already outpacing whatever it was that the nursing team had begun to put in place, so that to begin with I found myself talking at cross-purposes, and unable to explain myself – 'We don't send carers,' said a kindly but puzzled young man, 'that's for social services.'

'But they said someone was coming – they said someone would help.'

'There are forms to fill in. There would be means testing. Does your father-in-law have savings? Does he own his own home?'

'Yes I think so, yes he does – they already sent a commode and a walking frame, and she said we could have carers when we needed them, you see.'

A pause. Then: 'It doesn't seem to be on the system yet.'

'You see, it's all happening so fast – he's becoming incontinent, and he has to get to hospital tomorrow, but we don't know how to move him.' As I spoke I found that I was observing myself, and deplored how I veered between insistence, compliance, and pleading – it was as if there were three women there at the table: the prophet certain of her prophecy, the good citizen, and the frightened child.

'Have you got a pen? Go and get a pen. Make a note:

these are the forms you'll need . . .' When all this caused me, in the end, to be capable of little more than a helpless and baffled wail – there was no time for forms, or for assessments; he was already going out of our reach – I must at last, and without any skill on my part, have hit on the right form of words.

'Oh,' somebody somewhere said, and I heard down the line a faint but definite softening which was like a change of season: 'oh, I see. Yes, I see.' And later that same morning the same woman from the nursing team returned to us, and sat on the bed where she had sat before, and surveyed David for a time without speaking. Not a full day had passed since she'd seen him last and grasped his foot through the fading floral quilt; but the man she looked over now was not that same man. Her manner altered, because he was altered; she spoke to him only once, because she saw it was really no use: he could respond with nothing but a gentle confused smile that rose very slightly to the surface of his face, and then receded down to the private ruminations that took him over more and more, and which we were never able to comprehend.

'Can he stand?'
'Only if we're both here to help him.'
'Can he make it to the bathroom?'
'I don't think he can.'
'Is he drinking?'
'Sometimes, but he can't seem to hold the cup.'
'And is he in pain?'
'We ask, and we ask, and he says no.' I was wringing

my hands; Robert was sometimes in the hall, and sometimes at the door, because it was difficult for him to stand witness.

'He's very poorly, isn't he?' She made a note. 'What I am going to do,' she said, 'is fast-track David to end-stage care'; and this form of words, which evidently was so meaningful to her, meant very little to me. 'Later today,' she said, 'a hospital bed will come. That will make it easier for him to get up, and to lie down again. And carers will come, twice a day: they will help wash him and turn him, and show you how to do it. It is happening fast,' she said, and I felt such gratitude that it felt like love; and this was not because she was sending help, but because she saw what I'd seen. 'It is fast,' she said, 'it is really quite the change'; and when shortly afterwards she left, she did not exactly embrace me, only as she went by me in the narrow hall her body seemed to meet mine with affectionate purpose, and with assurance, as if she'd been one of those women who'd come that morning to tell me I could do what needed to be done – that in fact this was all, in its way, really quite run-of-the-mill.

﹏

In the fifteenth century, and in the time of plague, two texts by unnamed Dominican priests on how a man ought to prepare for his death were widely translated from their original Latin, and published in their tens of thousands across Western Europe. These were known as the *Ars Moriendi*, or *The Art of Dying*; and often they were illustrated with woodcuts showing the dying man attended on the one hand by saints and angels ringed in light, and on the other by capering devils signifying faithlessness and despair. In 1917 – when the European plague was not a flea-borne sickness, but a war – a woman named Frances Comper translated these manuscripts into English (difficult and loving work which, as she once wrote to T. S. Eliot, entailed 'much drudgery and little financial gain'), and published them as *The Book of the Craft of Dying*. 'All a city should come together with all haste to a man that is nigh death or dying,' it reads; 'what hour that ever it be, and where that ever they be – all things being left, hastily come.'

I suppose it is the crafts of birth and dying that change least with time, because it was as if, in the hours and days that followed, word had gone out across the city: people really did hastily come. After the woman had left us for the second time, we set about preparing the living room for the promised bed. The tapestry chair – which still had on it the imprint of David's body, and crumbs dropped from the last meal he'd eaten there – was carried out into the garage, where very quickly it mouldered alongside his lawnmower, and the packets of seeds for green beans he'd set aside for spring. We took the book of unfinished puzzles, the basket of stamps and the unopened post from the coffee table with its inlaid tiles, and pushed it against the wall; we found his slippers of beaten-down suede, and – imagining, if not quite believing, that he'd never need them again – we kept them to one side.

When, after no more than an hour or two, the bed did come, it was brought by those same men in those same monogrammed shirts, and carried out of that same van; they seemed not to have remembered that they'd seen us the previous day, only set the bed up with their cheerful efficiency and assured us, as they left, that they'd collect it as soon as we didn't need it any more. 'Put it where he can see the garden,' we said, 'put it where he can look out'; so we moved aside the lamps and curtains that would have obscured his view, and brought the tubs of flowering red geraniums inside, and put them on small tables by the window.

The bed was an engine for dying in. It was so large it displaced the air in the room. It was high, broad, and made of white painted metal; the mattress was deep, and covered in blue fabric that could be easily wiped down. It had a footboard of some shiny laminated material that did a poor job of imitating wood; a kind of table on a bracket, made of the same material, could be swung across the patient's lap or moved aside. A system of hydraulics concealed in the painted metal struts could raise the bed at the patient's head and at their knee; the mattress was filled with air, and moved very subtly at all times to prevent pressure sores. The controls for the bed were simple, with buttons set into a kind of white plastic lozenge that would sit comfortably in an invalid's palm; movements were indicated with arrows and images of the bed in altered positions, and this control could be clipped to the frame of the bed and extended on a coiled wire. If for some reason the bed became unplugged, a warning would sound; and afterwards, when we took out the plug because the sound of the air passing through the mattress was eerily like that of someone taking uneven shallow breaths, the high, thin note of alarm sounded like the wail of a hired mourner at the funeral of a stranger.

Meanwhile David lay for the last time in his own bed, often with his hand resting on one of the dogs, who out of laziness or loyalty would not be shifted from his side. I saw transformations in him which seemed not exactly to be signs of sickness, but of an extraordinarily rapid ageing, as if his malady was not cancer, but time. The wrists which extended from the blue cotton cuffs of his pyjamas were slender and white, the wrist-bones high and large enough to cast a shadow; when he smiled, as he often still did, there was not enough depth in his cheek to summon his dimples. His white hair, which had taken on the downy look of a dandelion clock, was thinner than I'd taken it to be, and when he moved his head against the pillow, light sometimes struck his scalp. Once, when he needed to urinate, we brought forward the commode, and having fumbled for a time with that unwelcome and unfamiliar thing we lowered him on to the seat, where he grasped the arms and sighed as he relieved himself of a startling volume of pale, weak urine – and I discovered that the promise of those vanished women who'd visited me briefly the previous day had not been empty after all: it was no trouble, it was not even surprising, to find myself cleaning and dressing him again, and carrying the brimming bowl across the hall to empty it into the toilet. That was all ordinary – it was the way of all flesh, and eventually would be the way of mine.

Towards the middle of that afternoon the first of the carers came. We never thought to ask exactly which organisation had sent them, and it was months later that I understood they'd come from the Norfolk Hospice, and that this hospice is largely funded by donations (so you see: the city, hearing that a man was nigh death or dying, had come quickly). In time, a kind of ecstatic exhaustion overtook Robert and me and made us stupid, and because of this the carers became more or less indistinguishable from each other, though there were young men and old men, young women and old women, accents from Eastern Europe and West Africa and Norfolk and London. But differences of sex and nationality were insignificant against the kinship of their profession, which seemed like family resemblance: they all came into the bungalow with authority and good humour, hanging up their winter coats and asking where they would find a clean bowl, a flannel and a towel; their conversations with David were always poised exactly between a kind of bolstering encouragement, and what often sounded like love. That first afternoon, their task was to move David to his deathbed; and I think if this had been done with any indication of the enormous significance of the thing, it would have been impossible to witness, perhaps even impossible to carry out: never again would he put his feet on that bedroom carpet, or cross that narrow hall where he'd laid down cheap mats for the sake of the dogs; never again look in the morning through the bedroom curtains, which were still new, to the bungalows over the road – never again see the parrots on the wall, the red numbers of the alarm-clock radio, the pine chest of drawers containing socks he'd washed, paired, and would never wear. But as they brought him – held and coaxed between them, unsteady on his feet – to the hospital bed, their conversation ('What would you like us to call you, Mr Perry? All right then, love, we'll call you David') fended off the enormity of what they were doing, and made it ordinary. So Robert and I left them to it, standing in the kitchen drinking tea, and listening as the carers raised from David murmurs and exclamations that contained, even then, his David-ness – 'Yes,' we heard him say, 'that's excellent, very good, yes. *Heh! Heh!*'; and when it transpired that one of those women had been born and brought up not far from Harlesden, where he'd lived with his parents and brothers, the voice which all that day had been vague and distracted strengthened suddenly, and the two entered into some conversation we couldn't make out, but which seemed to entail a fierce and cheerful competition about which of them could be most truly considered a Londoner. Then we were summoned in, and found David's hair combed, and his drawn face pink and shining from the flannel which lay folded over the rim of a bowl of soapy water, and his body covered in the faded floral quilt, and in a grey blanket of faux fur which he'd bought the previous winter for the dogs.

'Now,' said the woman from Harlesden to me, 'if you

need to change him before we come again, you will need to do it like this.' And she showed us how to roll David's compliant body towards us, and keep it resting against our own bodies as a sheet was quickly tugged out from under him, then quickly replaced; and how to gently but with authority roll him back towards the wall, and bring the sheet taut towards the other side. 'Ask them,' she said, 'for a WendyLett sheet,' and explained that this was a cleverly designed piece of fabric which would slide without friction up and down the mattress, and so make it easier to move David from place to place. 'You need incontinence pants, too,' she said, 'or pads: sometimes it's easier to find the puppy pads people use before their dog is house trained,' without suggesting in either her tone or her expression that there was anything shameful in these things, so that I was able to say, quite equably, 'Yes, of course,' and make a note. Meanwhile David, resisting for a time the private exhaustion which more and more overtook him, was both present and not present: biddable, quiet, allowing himself to be moved; if he felt any embarrassment keeping it to himself, for our sake. Then the woman addressed him, and handed him the white lozenge of the bed's controls. 'You'll need to get the hang of this, David,' she said. 'It will make things much easier, for when you need to get to the toilet and so on' (though I looked at her then, and wondered if she suspected, as I did, that he'd never again be on his feet). David took the controls from her with an intent but puzzled expression, as if he were returned to the May & Baker laboratories where he'd worked and some chemical compound was failing to behave as it ought to have done. For a brief time they played with the buttons, as she explained that his head should be raised a little, and so should his knees – it wasn't good for a man in his condition, at this time, to be laid flat – and though she seemed satisfied, returning the controls to the clasp on the bed's metal frame, I saw on David's face an irritated bemusement, because it had become beyond him to make sense of the symbols, or even to grasp that the bed he was in was not his own.

Soon after this they were gone, and while he was half-drowsing, David needed again to urinate, but was unable to say so in time for us to bring forward the commode, and manipulate the bed to bring him upright and on to his feet, which in any case I had been dreading. 'Oh,' he said, a little irritated with himself, as he soaked his pyjamas and the sheets; and I thought again how much liquid there was coming out of him, when really he'd done little more than sip at squash and milk for two days. 'Bring me the bowl,' I said, 'and the flannel,' and washing David I thought how beautiful his legs were: slender and white and hairless as a girl's, though I'll never know whether they'd always been this way, or whether that, too, was an effect of the disease. Other changes in his body were startling, and the man I washed in the morning might not be the man whose hair I combed that afternoon: his stomach was diminishing hour by hour, leaving a curved crease that showed where it had previously been, like the high-tide mark on a coastal wall; the skin on his chest and back lost the pinkish flush of its blood supply and became the colour and texture of vellum parchment, so that his many moles and age-spots seemed significant and legible as marks made in ink. The framework of his skeleton, slowly being revealed, was beautiful, and the flare of his collarbone came to look like that of a woman; but despite this wasting I could see, in the breadth of his shoulders and the exact arrangement of his limbs, how much his body resembled Robert's, so that occasionally, and with a kind of prophetic grief, it occurred to me that I might one day do all that again.

The effort of being cleaned and dressed tired him, and tired us — curiously there was a sense that we'd all had enough of each other, in the way families do towards the end of Christmas. Robert — who still had that new shy way of looking at his father, or not quite looking at him — tilted the television to ensure it could be seen from the high white bed, and found a snooker tournament; then for a time he drifted between the kitchen and the living room, speaking to David as if it had been any Saturday afternoon when he was young and those were the days when everyone watched the snooker, and his father would ask if he'd heard of that remarkable Russian player, Inoff the Red (*Heh! Heh!*). That evening — as David receded from us into a sleep that was strangely active, as if he were investigating himself — Jude came to the bungalow with dinner. Until then we hadn't realised we'd more or less lived off tea and biscuits for two days, and the food when we saw it changed the atmosphere of the kitchen, which was small and lit unpleasantly with a yellowish overhead light: briefly it might have been any other evening when we sat eating and talking with friends. She'd thought to bring dessert, and I remember it clearly – a bowl of lemon posset, and the ginger biscuits she often made, brought wrapped in brown paper – and I remember too how astonished I felt that even under those conditions the sight of good food could still give us pleasure. To begin with this caused me to feel guilty and ashamed, but soon I understood that it was because in fact death was already being accommodated in life.

Meanwhile the prospect of fitting the stent, which had been held before us as a kind of sacred ritual that would return the life force to a starving man, began to seem to us an impossibility. We looked at David as he drowsed in the hospital bed – night by then: the snooker tournament over, the winter-flowering almond hardly visible across the dark lawn – and saw the rims of his eye sockets now plain around the full circuit of his eyes, the wishbone curve of his naked legs, and could not imagine conveying that frail thing across the city, to be changed into a split-backed hospital gown and laid out under harsh lights to be, as he would have put it, interfered with. But then again, as we'd said over and over, he was a starving man, and that was half the trouble – if only he could take some nourishment we'd see the old face we recognised decently covering the planes of his skull. But towards the end of that day, as I began the night watch, Sam happened to text and ask how things were. And since he asked not only with the kindliness of a friend but with a doctor's tutored interest, it was possible to say that though David was safe, as the consultant had promised he'd be, we were worried, because in the morning we'd have to find a way to get him to hospital for the fitting of the stent, and didn't see how it could be done. Besides that, it seemed to us a monstrous thing to attempt: David by now was drifting in and out of lucidity, and there were times it would be difficult even to explain to him where he was being taken, and why. Then Sam asked if he could call, and when he did there was that same disconcerting combination of the familiar and unfamiliar which had struck me when I spoke to my sister, and her soft voice had been toughened with authority – 'Is it all right,' he said – in the quiet grave way I knew, but altered, so that I became at the same time biddable and comforted – 'if I speak to you plainly?'

'Please,' I said, 'please do' – because for a long time I'd felt that we were being too gently handled.

'He isn't dying because he is starving,' he said, 'he is dying because of the cancer'; then he went on speaking for a time, and I listened – all the while looking at Robert nearby, and noting the sighing noise of air moving in the mattress under David as he slept. 'It may not help,' said Sam, 'not now; and you see, he might not come home.' That was our thought too, I said, it had been our thought for a long time now; but it was difficult to speak or even to think against what we'd been told in a consultant's office, and by nurses who'd seen it make all the difference in the world. 'But I just think he's dying, Sam,' I said. 'I think even if we could get him there, it would be cruel.'

'Yes,' said Sam, 'I think so'; and then he explained what we should do – that in the morning, and at exactly half past nine, we should call the ward that was expecting us, ask for the senior nurse, and tell them we felt David was too frail to be moved. In time, Robert and I came to look on that conversation as if it had been a pause before the road diverged, and went two ways; and that because of Sam we carried David down the path we ought to have taken – and I have thought, too, that this kindness has given me a debt of gratitude I can't ever hope to repay.

Now it is the small hours. They are intimate: there is the impression of being in communion with other homes across the city, wherever lights are on and somebody isn't sleeping. We are alone with David, and watch over him in two-hour shifts (in the morning, a carer will laugh fondly and say we've made ourselves far too tired: we should sleep four hours each, and so divide the night in half). The carers when they came laid him out on his back and cradled by every pillow in the house; but he can never seem to keep himself there, preferring always to topple to his left, and with his knees drawn slightly up to his chest. It doesn't occur to me until then to notice that the bed has no side rail, and that after all David is not safe: as he topples, he comes nearer and nearer the edge of the bed, and his newly attenuated arms dangle over the side, sometimes grasping the struts on which the bed's controls are clipped; his head, left unsupported, will sag despondently over the carpet. Repeatedly I lift and move him on to his back and more safely against the wall, astonished at the weight of a body which seems smaller by the hour, as if he were getting further and further away: I try to be gentle, but gentleness can't move him. In the end there's nothing to be done but to draw the room's remaining armchair near the bed, and sit for an hour with my father-in-law cradled in my arms, until Robert wakes and comes to relieve me. When he does, he thinks of a solution, which is his way: we take the heavy coffee table and push it against the bed, then heap it with whatever cushions come to hand, forming a kind of supplementary mattress for David's head and shoulder to rest on.

It is the death watch. In the summer, in buildings where there's timber, the death-watch beetle ticks to attract its mate, and will go unheard unless for some reason somebody is awake; so it comes to be associated with quiet nights at the deathbed and mistaken for an omen. In Poland, a candle blessed at a February mass will be decorated with spiritual symbols or with flowers wrapped in ribbon, and lit when there are storms to ward off the lightning: this is the *gromnica*, the thunder-candle, and it is also lit at the deathbed for the final storm. There are no familiar rituals for us. We have no candles to hand, no songs passed down from our grandmothers; nobody ever said: when the time comes to keep vigil by a dying man, this is what you must do. It leaves us at a loss. Since I have no beads to tell, no black cloth to drape over David's bathroom mirror with its toothpaste splashes, I pass the time by parcelling the hours up into quarters:

in fifteen minutes I will check my phone, in fifteen minutes I can have a cup of tea. When I go to the kitchen to find something to eat, I discover David's cupboards are filled with Wagon Wheels – biscuits I've never seen him eat, but which he seemed to have hoarded in the weeks before he became visibly and irredeemably sick (later, Robert and I will discover that we each eked out those Wagon Wheels in the coming nights, so that they have now taken on for us the significance of soul cakes, the spiced biscuits that were once handed out on All Souls' Eve in remembrance of the dead). As we each watch alone, David sleeps; and only once, in a startling bellow, gives out one of his wordless and indecipherable cries. It is four days until he will die.

The following morning, before the carers came, Robert and I stood beside David's bed as again – and with an apology for getting in a muddle – he urinated where he lay. By then every sheet he owned had been laundered, and was hung out to dry on radiators and over doors: the smell of urine was almost displaced by the smell of washing powder. So we searched the cupboards and found the block-printed tablecloth we'd given him for Christmas, because he liked beautiful things, and because it was like the cloths we put on our own table when he came to us to eat. As we rolled him back and forth as we'd been taught, that cloth became emblematic to me of the speed and strangeness of his fall – that of course it could never have occurred to me, when I'd wrapped it in gold paper printed with holly leaves, that when I saw it next it would be making do as a sheet on a deathbed.

When he was dry and comfortable again, and had drunk half the glass of orange squash which Robert helped guide to his mouth, he had a long period of cheerful lucidity, when he kept out of the private exhaustion into which he'd increasingly retreat as if it were another room we weren't allowed to enter.

'Dad,' said Robert, speaking in the way he'd always spoken to his father – a courageous practice he maintained almost until the end – 'do you remember they said they'd give you a stent, to help you eat?'

'Yes,' said David. 'Yes, that's right.'

'Well, the appointment is for this morning, in a couple of hours.'

'Today?' – he considered this, and evidently was surprised it had come so soon; then he frowned, and together we silently assessed the practicality of the thing.

'Do you think you're strong enough?' I said, intervening, and thinking again what a responsibility it was to try to leave David in his own hands – or at least to let him think we were, when really the decision had been made. 'Do you think you'll be able to do it: to be up and dressed, and in the car? We can use a wheelchair again, of course we can – but we're worried it will be uncomfortable and difficult, and you might prefer to stay here.' Perhaps I ought to have said: and then, you see, you will starve.

'Oh,' he said, 'I'm not sure,' and frowned for a long time over the problem, which I recognised as the same indecision he sometimes showed when deciding which day of the week would be best for a visit to Yarmouth, or to the gardens we admired together when the weather was fine. 'I'm really not sure,' he said.

'Do you think it's best to stay here,' said Robert, 'at home, where you preferred?'

'I don't want to be messed about with,' said David, 'not really'; and all right, we said, all right, we would make the call, trying not to betray by our expressions how difficult this was, and how immense.

Then as Robert sat with his father and put on the morning news, and they talked the headlines over in almost their ordinary way, I did as I'd been told to do. At nine thirty exactly – having sat unmoving for minutes beforehand, watching the clock – I called the hospital department where we'd been instructed to take David, and asked if I could speak, please, to the senior nurse. She was brought quickly to the phone, and I knew from her voice and the warmth of her manner that this was the older of the nurses who'd sat with us in the consultant's office, and said with all the authority of her years and skill that a stent had often transformed patients almost beyond belief. So I was afraid that I'd be unable to explain that within three days it had become apparent that David couldn't be moved from where he was, and that it would be against both his interests and his wishes to do anything to him at all.

'I'm going to stop you there,' she said – I suppose she'd heard the fear in my voice, and the way I'd been preparing myself to do battle – 'I'm going to take this out of your hands. This is my decision: David shouldn't come in.

It would be difficult and uncomfortable for him, and he ought to stay at home. There, now: this is on me, and not you.' I remember I wept then, and was never able to thank her as coherently as I ought to have done. She understood that the chance of an extension to this one man's one life was being removed; but that he would not now die on a ward, surrounded perhaps by strangers if by anyone at all, and with no sight for example of a winter almond flowering a few yards past the foot of his bed. Often I think how those who helped us carried out duties which for them were impersonal, skilled, and perhaps forgotten by the evening – but which were of mortal significance to David, and to us: a gap too dizzying to contemplate.

In the coming days I sometimes doubted what we had done, and there was a night when I shut myself away and wept with guilt because David by then was refusing not only food but drink – 'We are starving him,' I said, 'that's what we are doing,' and the burden felt intolerable. But in fact it was not starvation that day by day refined him back to his marvellous bones, but the cancer itself, devouring him – as I said to myself at the time – like a pack of wolves; a metabolic process they call cachexia, during which the body's muscle mass is relentlessly and speedily consumed. Occasionally, when I saw the curiously active drowsing into which he increasingly fell, it occurred to me that he was dying because something in him resolutely lived, or approximated living – the cancer cells, rapidly doubling, and never like an ordinary cell maturing to carry out a purpose, but remaining permanently arrested in a kind of stupidly fertile and vigorous youth.

On that day, so many people came and went that the atmosphere in the bungalow became busy and companionable, like other days in other homes, when preparations were being made for a wedding, or the arrival of a new baby. I'd called for incontinence pads and pants, and they hadn't yet come; so Luther – ministering to David's body as well as his soul – arrived with his arms full of soft plastic packages of what we needed, and which we stored on the brick hearth where they were always close to hand. Together Robert and I learned to fit and remove disposable pants frilled with blue elastic, because it couldn't be done alone; and though the act itself caused me no embarrassment I resented how often it called to mind the times I'd changed a baby's nappy: that thought seemed in some way to outrage David's dignity. And I understand now how grateful I ought to be to him, for how readily and without shame he submitted to our nursing him, when all his life he'd been diffident and shy, and had only ever shown his love for Robert with a handshake. In *Bluets*, Maggie Nelson writes of tending to a friend severely and permanently injured by an accident, and who permits Nelson to see and even to participate in her pain: 'This is generous,' she writes, 'for to be close to her pain has always felt like a privilege to me.' David, I think, was generous in his sickness, and quickly learned the craft of dying: he allowed us to nurse him, never fending us off, or thinking himself diminished and humiliated by it – and possibly understanding, even then, that it was our privilege.

On that day, too, David was more or less himself,

whenever he wasn't sleeping. He was glad to see Luther, and glad to have him read from the Psalms; glad, too, when others came who shared his faith, and sat with him without seeming to betray, at least until they passed me in the hall on their way out, their shock at his condition. Again and again I returned with my phone to the dining table, and to the sheet of paper that told me WHO TO CALL?, trusting in the powers of the community hub and explaining that the bed had no rail, and that we needed something called, I thought they said, a Wendy-Lett sheet, was that it? That no, David was no longer eating, but no, he didn't seem to be in pain; that yes, we'd be pleased to see the district nurse. There were different nurses at different times, briefly attending us in their varying uniforms of varying blues. They spoke with David, satisfying themselves that he was at least safe, and not in pain or distress. Like the carers, these nurses seemed in due course to merge into a single entity, because of their shared manner, which was of skilled and impersonal kindness – though, I remember, one woman haltingly explained at the threshold of David's room that she didn't do dogs, and so Janey and Ruby – by now keeping watch from the floor, since they could no longer reach the bed – were hustled into the garden, and watched in despair from just beyond the doors.

That afternoon, we were shown how to tilt the bed to ensure David's bare feet weren't pressed against the footboard, which in time would cause pressure sores. 'What you need,' the carer said, 'is barrier cream: make a note, and get some for tomorrow, or as soon as you can.

Do you see how his mouth is becoming dry? You can get something called artificial saliva – write this all down.' I hadn't seen his bare feet against the board, or noted that his mouth was dry, and I'd never heard of such a thing as artificial saliva; left to me, I thought with a kind of panic, he'd be suffering, because I don't know what to do. Then they asked David if they could remove his false teeth (they didn't say: you don't need them, Mr Perry, not any more) and when they did, I was nauseated to see they were yellowish and furred with deposits – evidence of a kind of listless self-neglect which plainly had been going on for some time, and which had passed us by, so that I found myself apologising to them, as if I ought to have been cleaning them myself. With the dentures gone, there was nothing to maintain the structure of his face; and minute by minute, as it seemed, I watched his lower lip fold further inward over the toothless gum, so that by the following day – as his skin became thinner and more pale – it had the look of a pleated piece of white satin that for some reason he was keeping in his mouth.

That night – as we watched over David in shifts, coming forward again and again to hold his drooping head and shoulders in our arms, because there was still no side rail for the bed – there were changes in him which seemed to efface almost completely the David we knew, and replace him with a changeling creature. His skin was altered from the opaque and greyish putty which had frightened us the day we saw death in the market square: now it was creamy and almost poreless, with a curious sheen as if he were perspiring in droplets too small to be seen. His lips were folded very deeply in; his cheeks, which had always been round, now fell from the broad structure of his face with a drape like cloth, and it was possible to see the divots of the skull at his temples, and the hard rim at the outer part of his eyes; even his snub nose seemed to be refined and pared back. The effect was to transform him from a man who'd always had the comfortable, oaky look of an English peasant into something mythic, all pathos and gravity. And it was that night, as I diligently portioned out the minutes between bites of Wagon Wheel or sips of tea, that he began to bellow again in his sleep, and I understood – as if I'd been slow to learn his language – that in fact he was communicating something, to us or to God or to himself: it was not after all wordless, as I'd taken it to be – he was crying out 'No! No!', then 'Oh dear . . .', and 'Why . . . why?' Nothing in those days ever distressed me more, and when I think of it now a cold wind passes over me – I went quickly to the bed to rouse him, or try to; but when eventually he opened his eyes and registered my presence, and that I was saying, 'Are you in any pain, Dad? Does something hurt?', he said, 'No, I'm all right. I'm all right,' in a vague way, as if he couldn't think why I'd woken him; then he drifted again into a sleep that for the rest of the night was quiet.

I have said that it seemed we were all retaining our essential selves – that David kept his David-ness, and

Robert his Robert-ness, as if our characters were fixed and finished, and not altered by circumstances. But I've always disliked the Shakespeare sonnet quoted so often at weddings that it's become as cheap as daffodils, that 'love is not love, which alters when it alteration finds'. I think an intelligent and responsive love has the humility to change with circumstance, in the way a high bridge will be made to bend and not break in bad weather. There was once a poet and priest who lived all his life in Wales, in circumstances of poverty and self-denial that he inflicted on his wife (forbidding her to use a vacuum cleaner for example, since he found the noise distracting), and who died at home at the age of eighty-seven of a bad heart, his face in old age having the grim but sacred look of an exhausted pilgrim. This was R. S. Thomas, whose lyric verse very nearly saw him awarded the Nobel, and whose poetry I love for its strange and almost bitter faith. In his poem 'Cures', he writes of a Cathar woman named Guillemette, who was investigated by the Spanish Inquisition, and who is supposed to have said: 'My poor friend, my poor friend, the soul is nothing but blood.' I've thought of that often in the years since David died, and wondered if Guillemette understood something that had passed me by – that perhaps a soul is not carried around in the indifferent, irrelevant vehicle of the body, but that the two are united, and so a change in the body will also change the soul.

I wonder this because as David's body changed, his essential nature also seemed to change. Hour by hour his diffidence and his occasional tendency to sharpness and irritation were being refined away, and he became sweeter, in a way he might I suppose have been as a boy, before he'd been strained by life. Towards the end, there was a time I roused him because I needed to tell him the nurse had come; and I watched his muddled gaze rove distractedly about before fixing on mine. Then, as he registered slowly that it was my face held close to his, a light came into his eyes which I've really only ever seen before in young babies – as if he were suddenly seized with a wordless but entirely comprehending kind of love; then briefly he smiled, and after that the light receded like a coin dropped in a dark pond. And since he changed, I also changed. I'd never before used any term of endearment for him – we weren't that kind of family, and he wasn't that kind of man. But soon I found myself calling him sweetheart, darling – words which would have been unthinkable only a week before – because now I felt for him the easy and entirely unembarrassed love I have for babies: so 'All right, my love,' I said to him, rolling his body away from soaked sheets, or guiding his hands to a mug of orange squash. 'All right, sweetheart. They're coming. Somebody will be here soon.'

Later that morning, when the carers did come, we brought them the artificial saliva they'd asked for, and the WendyLett sheets which had by then been delivered, and which constituted two large pieces of fabric, fitted with handles and woven in a particular way which allowed us to move David without hurting his body, or ours – so we marvelled over this loving ingenuity, which seemed at that moment as transformative and necessary as steam power. 'And we found the barrier cream,' I said, wanting, as I've always wanted, to be the good pupil, 'to stop the pressure sores from coming on his feet.'

'Oh, no,' said the carer, examining the white plastic tub with her expert's eye, 'no,' she said, 'they've given you the wrong thing: this is emollient cream, not barrier cream – this won't do it.'

'I'll go now,' said Robert, 'I'll go straight away.'

'It's all right, sweetheart,' said the carer. She put down the tub. 'It's all right,' she said, 'you stay here. I don't think he's going to need it'; and though she said this gently and without emphasis, we understood what she meant: that he'd never develop sores on his feet, because he wouldn't have the time.

After the carers had gone – a fine, fair day; the geraniums faring well enough indoors – we found David alert and wanting to talk, and for a while the three of us sat easily going over the years and making each other laugh. Robert remembered that when he was young, and the family would sit at the oval dining table with its rubbed varnish having their breakfast (artificially sweetened tea; Sugar Puffs; toast and marmalade), his carefully expressionless father would move his body during the Shipping Forecast, sinking into his seat whenever the announcer intoned that the pressure was falling, and then sitting straight again at 'rising', counting the years until Jenny noticed and understood the connection. And when in the end she did understand, she'd said, 'Oh David! And all this time I thought you were just being silly!' He often referred to that famous novel *All Smallers Great and Creach*, knowing perfectly well the joke was appalling and for that reason only finding it funnier; when *The Archers* theme tune struck up on the radio, he'd sing 'What a load of filthy muck! What a load of rubbish!', with the genial sense that he was grateful to the BBC for giving him something to complain about. Since his silliness seemed to resist all his exhaustion, it occurred to me that I could read something funny to him (though it occurred to me, too, that perhaps I was only emulating what ought to be done at a deathbed). So I fetched his Folio Society edition of *Three Men in a Boat*, which all night had overlooked our mattress on the floor, and which he'd lent me once when I was miserable from tonsillitis, and laughed helplessly despite the laughter searing my throat. For a time I sat cross-legged beside his bed, the dogs sleeping behind me and the sun beginning to go down, and read the first chapter or so, while David lay propped on his pillows with his eyes shut, evidently following the absurd tale and laughing often in his old way – *Heh! Heh!* – sometimes in anticipation of the lines he knew were coming.

Perhaps half an hour after this, David's pain began. The laughter ended. He withdrew from speaking to us; he began to refuse even sips from the cups of water and squash we tried to give him, and receded into the half-drowsing and almost secretive state which more and more had been taking him over. But now he did this with frowns and groans, and reaching behind himself to pat distractedly at his back, as if it had been one of the dogs – 'Dad,' we said, coming together to the bed, 'does it hurt? You must tell us, if you have pain.' We'd asked and asked, and he'd denied it, and perhaps we ought not to have believed him; but now – reluctantly, and with the look of resigning himself to an unpalatable truth – he said that it did hurt, a bit, in his back. And it struck me that there'd perhaps been pain there for days, and that this was why he'd been taking up that same position whenever he could: lying curled like a child on his left, because he couldn't bear the pressure of the bed against his back. We called for the nurses then – 'It's changing,' I said, 'he has pain now, can somebody come? Please can somebody come soon?'

Often when I think of those days, I'm unable to believe – or even comprehend – the impossibly opposed incidents and sensations they contained. It is true, and astonishing to me even now, that I never baulked at the intimacies of nursing, or the disintegrations of a body preparing itself for the grave – all that became quite ordinary, and caused me no more difficulty than cleaning my own teeth. But at the same time, and with equal conviction, I often thought to myself that I'd never in my life seen anything so sad – the slow deliberate movements David made as he reached with both hands for a blue-flowered mug of water, the sight of his empty slippers in the corner of the room, Robert's courageous attempts – even in the small hours; even when the man in the bed had taken on a stranger's face – to speak to his father as he'd always spoken to him, so that he'd never lose his son. Comedy and tragedy passed through the bungalow like a troupe of players that couldn't make up its mind. One afternoon, at a time of solemn and contemplative quiet as the visiting pastor bowed his head in prayer, the washing machine – which was rarely out of use – announced the end of its cycle by playing tinnily, and apparently in its entirety, the melody of Schubert's Trout Quintet, so that even Luther was hard-pressed to maintain his poise before he could say his amen. But within the hour, the idea that we might ever laugh again, or in fact ever have laughed at all, seemed absurd, as the remorseless disease and the shock of its speed occurred to us as if for the first time. Now and then I became disembodied, looking on in disbelief from some unswept corner of the ceiling, in the way I'd only experienced before at times of heartbreak, or prolonged and extraordinary pain. One afternoon I opened David's post, and knelt by his bed to read aloud a card sent from old friends in Essex. It had been written and posted on a day when David could still dress himself, if only wearily; by the time it was delivered he was no longer able to open an envelope. I read the note to him, and saw how pleased he was by the memories it contained of the times he'd spent with his friends; but when I came to the part where they said how they looked forward to seeing him again – which they never would, not at any rate on this side of Jordan – I was silenced by a painful tightness in my throat that was as disabling as the press of a spiteful hand, and resting my forehead against the white frame of the bed I cried noisily. All the while I was observing myself – the long, full-sleeved black dress I wore during most of that week, which was heavily embroidered and I suppose resembled a Victorian mourning gown; the absurdly tragic pose beside the bed – and thinking: get up, woman, get up off your knees, do you think you're in a novel? So what was funny existed alongside what was intolerably sad, and the process of dying struck us as both quite ordinary, really almost a household task, but also incomprehensibly strange – these things not cancelling each other out as they ought to have done, but persisting in undiminished quantities, like a failure of simple maths.

Once, when I was quite young and had never really experienced pain, an old man whose name I cannot remember told me how, when he was a child, a neighbour had taken a long time to die of cancer of the stomach, and that he'd heard the dying man's screams a few doors down, and how he'd begged for a gun. The memory of this haunted me for years, then diminished as memories do; but when David conceded that afternoon that his back had begun to hurt, and I understood why it was he'd taken to always lying on his side, it returned to me so forcibly that it made me tremble, and the wait for the nurse that night – as we sang to him, and smoothed lotion into his forearms in the hope the sensation might distract him for a time – was brief, but cruel. It was dark by then, and for two days I'd been confined to the bungalow as if on a voyage below deck: when I opened the door to the district nurse, who came quickly, the streetlights reflecting on the soaked pavements had the look of phosphorescent sea-creatures. This nurse was a man, red-headed and brisk, whose dark blue tunic gave him the air of a medicval page: whenever he came to the bungalow, which after that day was often, the air seemed to become charged with his efficiency and purpose. He went to David's bed – fitted, at last, with its side rail – and questioned him in an authoritative way that had more effect than mere kindness, though he was also kind: 'Now, David. Do you have pain?'

'Yes,' said David, speaking quite lucidly, but with incomplete sentences, as if it had become too tiring to speak in full. 'Yes, bit sore. Back' – he sighed as he spoke.

'It's your back that hurts, is it?'

'Little bit' – and it isn't a little bit, I thought.

'All right.' It seemed to me this nurse had seen a thousand men complaining of a thousand pains, and had assessed both David's condition and his habitual understatement at a look. 'All right,' he said – lightly he grasped David's shoulder through the grey furred dog blanket – 'we'll take care of that for you'; and leading us through to the kitchen stooped over the dining table and began to complete paperwork, explaining that it was time, now, to administer morphine injections, which would make David more comfortable. The nature of this medication required levels of authorisation I'd never seen before, and which I never fully understood, so that I became afraid to throw anything away, or even to tidy up, in case I dispensed with the solitary scrap of paper which would be all that stood between David and an easeful death. We were instructed to take the prescription to a pharmacy, and then return home with the morphine; then we were to phone the community hub, who would despatch a nurse to give the injection. So Robert headed out into the wet night, but perhaps that day women and men all over Norwich were dying or beginning to die, since he was gone a long time, visiting pharmacy after pharmacy before at last the fifth could supply what we needed. Meanwhile I stood beside David's bed, stroking the downy hair from his forehead and singing to him the old hymns we both knew by heart, and saying, 'It's all right, sweetheart, they're coming, my love. Somebody will be here soon.'

When Robert returned with the pharmacy's white paper bag, which seemed to us the most precious thing in the world, we waited for perhaps an hour before a nurse was able to come, so that I became unjustly and inconsolably angry, wondering aloud what these people thought they were doing and why they didn't care, and whether it would really matter if I attempted to draw up the injection and deliver it myself. Then the nurse did come – a woman rather older than me, dressed in pale blue and with fair hair drawn back to the nape of her neck with a rubber band – and having examined and amended the papers we gave her, she went into the room where David lay and returned, as it seemed, seconds later, having given an injection in his thigh. 'Thank you,' we said, 'oh, thank you'; seeing how quickly the tension eased from his forehead, which within minutes lost its troubled frowning look.

'Whenever he is uncomfortable,' she said, 'whenever you think he needs it: call' – then she went out into the night, leaving us to say how astonishing it was – really how unbelievable – that it was possible to speak to a stranger on the phone, and that this stranger would summon another stranger, who would come to administer a substance that would ease suffering in a moment, then quietly leave.

~

Towards the end of the third winter after David died, and towards the end of writing this book, it occurred to me that really I'd had very little idea of what Robert had been thinking during those nine days. I hadn't been watching him, or trying to decipher his words or the cast of his face as he stood beside the white metal bed, or set out yet again in his car in the night to fetch medication, or something to eat. This isn't because I wasn't interested, or didn't care, but because we were standing side by side and looking only and fixedly at his father. I'd seen how he had insisted on remaining David's son, as he'd always been; and how quite often when he first came into the room he'd avoid looking at the bed, because the man in it didn't much resemble the father he was speaking to when the snooker was on; but besides that I'd given him far less thought than I might usually have done. So as we walked one morning in a park near where we live, and saw with relief the snowdrops and aconites that showed winter was breaking into spring, I asked if he could remember how he felt in those days – when we decided not to take his father to hospital for the stent for example, or the times when Luther came and we watched him pray. 'What I felt,' said Robert then, 'was that Dad wasn't either fighting or not fighting, which is the kind of language they use for cancer, which now I see is all wrong. What I saw was that he submitted. It wasn't giving up. It was something better and maybe even braver than that. And I never doubted that we were right to keep him home, not once.' I'd doubted it sometimes, I said, and cried in the night because I thought he was starving, and that it was all our doing. 'But I knew him best,' said Robert, 'and I knew what he wanted. And all the time,' he said, 'I was thinking about how to be his son – or really, how to be a good son. On those nights when I sat up with him – eating all those Wagon Wheels, do you remember? – I was preparing for what I'd do after he was dead. Because I knew I wouldn't stop being his son just because he'd died. He would still be my dad. And I would still have to be a good son.' We went on walking, and I said I wondered how much David's faith had to do with that submission. 'Well, he would have thought he was going to see my mum, and his mum,' said Robert. 'And even though by then we didn't have the same faith as him, it felt as if believing what he believed was the same thing as wanting what he wanted. And perhaps that accounts for why he became more affectionate towards the end – sweeter, as you say. All his life he'd worried about things, been nervous about having to speak to people or make decisions, and all that was over. He never needed to make a decision again.'

'Were you ever afraid?'

'Oh, yes. But not of death, or what was happening to him. I was afraid of being alone. He was going to die, and then I'd have no parents, no siblings, no children. And I didn't know what that was going to be like.' I had no consolation to give him then, and felt it would have been wrong to try.

The same night the pain began, they sent us for the first time a night carer, so that Robert and I could sleep. They said he'd come at 10 p.m., and he was late. Often in those days my impatience was intolerable both to me and to everyone else, and I remember how maddened I was when at a quarter past ten there was finally a knock at the door; and I remember too how my impatience dissipated immediately into gratitude, as it always did as soon as help arrived. He was a tall, large man; his name was Emmanuel. At least: that is the name I remembered, and the name I've used whenever I've told this story since; and though recently I discovered that his name in fact was quite different, I'm still unable to think of him in any other terms. He had no uniform, only a white polo shirt and a pair of loose jeans; he carried a heavy rucksack. I offered him tea, which he accepted; then he went directly to the room where David lay in an easeful opiate sleep, and looked for a long moment, without any surprise or disquiet, at the dying man. He nodded once, quite solemnly, in greeting or understanding or both; then began to take food from his rucksack, and a weighty old laptop covered with stickers, which he opened on the coffee table. Robert and I, lingering in the hall, were uncertain what we should do: for five days and four nights we'd neither slept nor been away from David's side for more than two or three hours at a time, and it seemed remarkable and in fact indecent to think we could leave him in the hands of this stranger. But Emmanuel – looking up from the football match already playing on the laptop – saw us drifting with the dogs distractedly back and forth past the door, and said: 'You go to bed, he's all right with me'; and said it with such authority that with a kind of dumb gratitude we each kissed David goodnight, then lay down on our mattress on the floor – though fully dressed, because we thought we'd be needed in the night.

   I couldn't sleep; and so I passed the time by scrolling through images of the most luxurious and expensive clothes I could find, until my eyes were sore with wonder and avarice. I might have hoped I'd turn that night towards the sacred or the strange – I might have hoped I would pray for David, and for us all. But it seemed the proximity of death could do nothing to diminish my love of beautiful clothes, and every garment seemed to represent some future afternoon, or even hour, that would call for yards of satin and glasses of wine, not incontinence pants with their dispiriting blue elastic, and water in mugs that were easy to hold.

One thing in particular took hold of me, with the kind of longing I suppose a dedicated drinker might feel for a drink – an immense opera coat, cut with wide sleeves and a broad, high collar that folded back from the frail stem of the model's neck, and made of antique cloth. In the 1920s this cloth had been a kimono: it was a heavy, morning-blue silk, and embroidered by hand with the most elaborate stems of pale flowers resembling honeysuckle, on which butterflies had sometimes settled. The cuffs of this coat, and parts of the lining, were made from the pinstriped wool of a sombre gentleman's suit. I'd never seen anything so beautiful, still less owned it, and its cost ran to several months' mortgage – a cathedral of a coat, constructed over the course of a century by women and men who'd lived, and died, and were still living. All that night, and quite often in the day that followed, I returned again and again to that coat, saying to myself with childish determination that one day I'd have it, or at any rate something like it. And the following night, when I secretly examined it as I lay not sleeping on the mattress, I found its price halved as if someone had taken pity on me – and in fact there was no time for 'one day', I thought; I might already have a tumour in my breast or my liver, that was already communicating with my bones – might perhaps be struck by a bus on a Wednesday afternoon when the days were short and dark. So in the dead of night, and with a *little pig, little pig* heart, I bought that coat, where I suppose I should have resolved to forgive my enemies, and give all my goods to the poor. It came to the house the day after David died, swaddled in layers of black tissue paper, and was larger and heavier than I'd thought it would be, so that to put it on felt like inhabiting a room. And when I wear it now – as I sometimes do – and am stopped in the street by strangers surprised by its beauty, I've learned not to say: 'I bought this, you see, because I was watching somebody die.'

―

There is in Jewish tradition a practice of attempting to trick the Malakh ha-Mavet: the Angel of Death, who as the Talmud says is 'full of eyes'. Say someone becomes so gravely ill you suspect the Angel of Death has entered their name on the ledger, you may formally change their name, and so in good faith turn the angel from the door: no, you're mistaken, nobody of that name lives or is dying here (it amuses me to think you can trick the Angel of Death, so long as you don't downright lie). 'Why is this night different from all other nights?' asks the youngest child at the yearly Seder feast, when Jews remember how Moses had the Israelites mark their doors with the blood of a lamb, so the Angel of Death would pass over them. I think of this now, when I think of those nights which were not like all the other nights, when we cradled David in our arms to prevent him falling from the bed, or measured out the night with Wagon Wheels. Did we ever think of death as an angel to be tricked, or fended off by pacts sealed with blood – did we ever hope it would pass over the bungalow? In those first days, when we both believed and doubted our own prophecies, I'd never thought of death as a being – no cowl and scythe, no angel full of eyes – but certainly it had seemed to me something cohered and substantial, which occasionally passed from our view then appeared again like a trickster at our heels. But I think none of us ever thought it could be dodged or outwitted – there was, as Robert later said, the sense that David had submitted to death, or at least accepted it, and because of that we accepted it too. And during those eight nights which were not like any other nights, it became impossible to think of death as an entity or an intelligence, or even as a shadow – it was simply an event, a thing that would happen, as inevitably as midnight follows eleven o'clock.

We slept that night more deeply than seemed decent, and woke drearily at sunrise. Stumbling together across the hall we found the door to the living room slightly ajar, and Emmanuel already putting away his laptop and the remains of his food: 'It was a good night,' he said, 'a quiet night'; and we went quickly to the bed and saw the dog blanket rising and falling with David's breath.

'Thank you,' I said. 'Thank you for helping us – and can you go home now, and sleep?'

'Not yet,' said Emmanuel, ruefully smiling and putting on his coat; then he explained that he had six children, and so really it had been a rest for him, to sit with David in the peace and quiet. 'I will see you again tonight,' he said; then looking backwards once at his charge in the bed, as if to check he was still where he'd left him, he went out.

That same day my parents came. My mother had called, and said they felt they should come, if we'd like that – to see David of course, who'd been their friend and family for twenty-five years, and to help us if they could. So I watched for them at the window like a loyal dog, and ran barefoot down the wet drive to greet them, reduced to a child again by the sight of my mother. She'd brought shepherd's pie in a heavy clay dish, painted with white flowers, which I recognised: I recognised the hair which waves like mine waves, the dress she wore, her shoes – I recognised my father, who seemed young and vigorous to me then, though he was older than David and had always looked it, too. They were miraculous to me, as if I'd been expecting a kind of universal degradation to have taken place while I wasn't watching; when I embraced them I felt as if I reached through a breach in time – that I was young again, and so were they, and perhaps so was David.

When they'd last seen him – late that summer, this was: the weather very fine; a trip to an aviation museum where we'd taken turns to sit in the fuselage of a military aircraft, while swing music played from the years they'd been born – his cheeks had been plump and faintly tanned, and his stomach had swelled comfortably as he'd eaten a cream tea he said was excellent, really excellent. So as I took them through to the room with its white engine of a bed, I felt that I took it all in for the first time, as they were taking it in – the coffee table with its mugs of water, and balls of cotton to moisten David's lips; the emollient cream which now we used to rub into his desiccating arms and hands, and the little white canister of Oralieve saliva substitute we now and then sprayed into his open mouth to prevent his tongue becoming painful and dry; the immense plastic packages of incontinence pads spilling on the hearth; and most startling of all David's new skin, made waxy with its poreless sheen, the hands which once might have been a labourer's hands now resembling those of a Russian pianist, as hour by hour he transformed into something that was at the same time both diminished and grand. 'Hello, David,' they said, coming forward and seeming less troubled than I might have expected them to be. My mother bent to kiss his cheek – 'It's very good to see you,' they said, and I noticed a kind of sweetness in the way they spoke to him, and which I'd never heard before.

'Oh!' said David, who'd not yet moved past recognising old friends. He called them by their names, he showed pleasure and surprise; slowly he moved his hand from under the covers to grasp theirs. Then they spoke for a while in their ordinary way, as Robert and I brought kitchen chairs into the room so that it was possible for us all to sit companionably together. By then we'd settled into tasks that we carried out almost without thought, and largely without distress. Twice a day the hospice carers came, and saw to it that David was clean, though in fact by then the constant urination had almost come to an end, because he was running out of himself (and it was on this day the blonde woman from the cleaning company looked up as she repositioned David, and caught my eye, and said: 'So it *is* you! I thought I recognised the name'). Frequently and by turns we dipped cotton balls into the blue-flowered mugs of water, and moistened his lips; we held the lightest cups we could find to his mouth and helped him to drink. We watched fearfully for signs of pain, and when they came I'd run to the dining table and summon help, and as we waited for the nurse to come we'd attend to him more closely, sometimes singing hymns because this would settle him, or we persuaded ourselves that it did. I noticed a curious pattern: when awake, David was tranquil and vague, responding with faint smiles which faintly resembled his old smiles, or a word or two to say that yes, he was comfortable; that no, he didn't want anything to drink. But when he slept, or seemed to, there was something more active and energetic taking place, his face expressive and querying and even sometimes troubled, his hands restless at his sides – as if, at those times, he'd already crossed a border we couldn't see, and was investigating a new and unfamiliar land.

It was I think that afternoon I realised it was a Sunday. All his life David had marked Sundays with church, and there'd been a Sunday morning – and a recent one – when he'd had his last service, and he'd had no idea: would not have known to look as long as he could at the arrangement of the chairs that day, the early light in late October, the coats of the men and women who sat in front of him. But it occurred to me that now we constituted more or less a congregation; and so I texted Luther and asked if he would please come to the bungalow, bringing hymnbooks with him, to hold a last service there. Thinking over that evening I wonder if I'm only telling stories to console myself, or to coax heat back into the chilling embers of my faith – it seems to me almost absurd that such grace could have attended David then, and attended us all. The trouble is of course that dead men don't tell tales, and it's left to the living to say to each other, uncontradicted: it was like this, and then it was like this. They say for example that Francis of Assisi, having heard for the last time 'The Canticle of the Sun' ('Praised be my lord for our sister the moon, and for the stars'), lay in perfect silence at sunset, then all at once was attended by a flock of birds that circled the house singing as he died. Well, perhaps; or perhaps he went to his end quite sulkily, and no birds sang.

Still: it was like this. Luther came to the bungalow in the evening with six hymnbooks. One each. He wore trousers and a white shirt, and over his shirt a light grey sweater. He went into the room where David lay half-conscious because of the morphine he'd been given, and also because he was dying. Luther greeted him. David registered his presence with a sighing smile; his head on the pillow rolled away from us all. My parents sat side by side overlooking the bed on chairs set against the wall: my father wore a shirt and tie as he always did, my mother wore a dress and cardigan. Robert and I sat on the dining chairs brought in from the kitchen; I cannot remember what we wore. There was another chair, which we put nearest the bed and gave to Luther. None of these chairs were comfortable. The light in there was dim. Outside in the dusk the pigeons moved in their private rituals between the rooftops and the lawn. Janey slept; Ruby now and then lifted a paw and asked to be loved. My parents had their Bibles with them. So did Luther. I couldn't think where mine was or when I'd seen it last. We began by singing, and though I don't remember that first hymn I recall what a relief it was that we sang it well enough. Sometimes David registered the music with movements of his head against the pillow, but it seemed to me that really he was elsewhere, and that if we reached him at all it would be only faintly, as if through a window half-open down the road. Luther prayed, then preached for a time in the sincere quiet way which was his ordinary speaking voice, and as he spoke David's body became a little restless under the cover of the faded floral quilt and the dog blanket, as if he'd been summoned reluctantly back into himself. He nodded vigorously several times, frowning in concentration, then opened his eyes and surveyed the preacher with comprehending pleasure – 'Encouraging,' he said, nodding again, 'encouraging!' Luther prayed; David frowningly attended to it, and heard the amen. Then I asked if we could end by singing a hymn which for days had been playing in that room, and which I hoped was familiar but not yet worn out – 'Great is thy faithfulness, oh God, my Father; there is no shadow of turning in thee' – and as we sang David was drawn more and more back from whatever unseen land he preferred to inhabit, and became absolutely present in the room with us. In chapel he'd always sung shyly and in fact rather out of tune; but his voice now was powerful, and becoming more certain of itself with each verse, and his recollection of the hymn's words was exact. As he sang he took his arms out from under the covers and raised them above his head, his wrists and hands pale and startling as bones, extending from cuffs of pyjamas which had become far too big, and which now fell vacantly back towards his elbows – he seemed almost to be conducting the music, or commanding us to sing, all the while singing himself, his eyes closed and an expression on his face that was a kind of relieved joy. At the last verse his hands dropped again to his sides, and he sighed and rolled his face away from us again on the pillow in a way that seemed to me to be final. We were quiet for a time. What could we have said? It was both the saddest and the most triumphal thing I'd ever seen. I collected the hymnbooks, which I'd often done in chapel when I was a child and wanted to be good; I watched Luther bend to kiss David's cheek. 'Thank you,' we said, 'oh, thank you'; and as I stood at the door and watched the pastor go, I thought for the first time that death wasn't something merely happening to David, but that in fact he was participating in it. He was always a shy man, and shy about taking his leave – when visiting us he'd announce his departure by following me aimlessly to the kitchen and back, or sitting abruptly upright and casting about for a form of words that eluded him. But now, as I think of his raised arms as we sang – the bones nearly bare under a drapery of skin, the hands long-fingered and white – I see not submission but resolve, and a faith as confident and frank as our trust that the sun will eventually rise. And since I can't persuade myself that the assurance and peace of the dying is the preserve of any single faith or philosophy, I think instead it may be a grace as available and common as the old, reliable sun. This is the Hindu poet Rabindranath Tagore, in *Gitanjali*, or *Song Offerings*:

> *I have got my leave. Bid me farewell, my brothers!*
> *I bow to you all and take my departure . . .*
> *A summons has come and I am ready for my journey.*
> *At this time of my parting wish me good luck, my*
>   *friends! The sky is flushed with dawn and my path*
>   *lies beautiful.*

~

David was never lucid again. When the hymnbooks and the pastor were gone, there was a brief period of quiet as he lay silent and grand as a figure on a tomb, his mouth open and the satiny pleats of his lower lip folded in, and the full circuit of his eye sockets showing around his closed eyes. Then – with a suddenness and power that startled us from the reverie – he raised himself on his elbows and began to look about with a gaze that was simultaneously searching and unseeing. He didn't speak, only articulated a kind of determined discomfort we were unable to decipher; then he threw back the covers and swung his legs towards the edge of the bed, where they audibly struck the safety rail; then grasping the rail with his left hand he tried to come to his feet. I ran forward, frightened and even I think a little nauseated by the sight, which seemed more unnatural than his lassitude – 'No, no,' I said. 'No, Dad – it's all right: you can stay there, you can stay where you are,' thinking perhaps he needed to urinate and wanted to make his way to the bathroom. This mollified him, and he allowed himself to be coaxed back against the pillows; but as soon as I began to draw the covers over him, he pushed them away with fretful irritated movements and began again to sit up. I thought how terribly compromised his body was – drained of its fluid, and starved for days; the cancer distributing through distant fibres of his matter from the site of that first tumour like a drop of black ink staining the full bowl of water; the fat and muscle gnawed within a week from his bones – and was desperately afraid he'd fall, and get some injury which would see him alone on a ward under unkind lights until he died. So I did battle with him, and again I found gentleness couldn't move him, because he was summoning up some horrible vigour: 'No,' I said, pushing at his shoulders with both hands, 'no, Dad: please, you must stay where you are.' Not since I was a child had I touched another body roughly, and even now it's intolerable to me to think what a violence it was to pit my strength against that of a dying man. Then Robert joined me, and I think it was as much his presence as his power that caused David suddenly to subside again on the high slope of his pillows – 'There you go, Dad,' said Robert, still maintaining his old familiar way of speaking, 'there you go.'

My parents, watching, said that perhaps he was in pain – perhaps the latest morphine injection had by now worn off; they too came forward and tended to him, speaking gently and consolingly, my mother smoothing at the white hair which had fallen forward as he moved. 'Is it pain, Dad,' we said, 'does it hurt?' – but it wasn't possible for him to say, and perhaps not even possible for him to know. So I ran again to the dining table, and the precious scrap of paper, and called for help – 'I don't know what's happening,' I said, 'he is trying to stand. He seems very strong, it's not easy to keep him safe – please will you come?' There passed perhaps half an hour of a kind of fellowship which is precious to remember, as all of us – together or by turns – attended devoutly to the man in the bed, whose body was tense and sometimes flinching with an unthinking purpose he was unable to communicate. Sometimes we sang to him, and my father over and over again dipped balls of cotton into a mug of water, and used it to moisten his lips; meanwhile Robert grasped his father's hand, or smoothed at the dog blanket: 'It's all right,' we said, 'it's all right.'

Then the red-headed nurse came and Robert ran to the door, explaining before he'd crossed the threshold what had happened and how troubled we were. This nurse went briskly through to the bed, examining meanwhile the charts that showed what medication David had been given, and when, and by whom – 'He won't be in pain,' he said, 'he is on enough morphine. I think this is what we would call terminal agitation,' he said, and explained that in some cases, and towards the very end, there were changes in the brain chemistry which caused a dying patient to become restless and startlingly strong. 'We can help,' he said – his manner was calm, but seemed to me then grimly purposeful – 'we can help with that.' Seated again at the table, he completed paperwork which Robert was to take as soon as he could to a pharmacy; then again we were to call and say the medication was in hand, and someone would return to the bungalow. But it was a Sunday, and late, and pharmacies were largely closed; and so I remember that night sitting for a long time on the solitary plastic chair in the solitary supermarket pharmacy that was open, crying with fear and frustration as the dispensing chemist sometimes and with sympathy met my eye. When at last we had what David needed, and the nurse had come quickly to administer it, we watched with a kind of frightened gratitude as the body under the blanket slowly stilled. I thought then how Sam had told me once that the words 'passion' and 'patient' have something in common, coming from the Latin verb *patior*, which is variously translated according to its context. It might mean 'to suffer' or 'to endure'; 'to bear' or merely 'to undergo'; and even 'to allow' or 'to permit' – so on one page it might call to mind lovers enduring their desire, and on the next the torment of Christ on the cross. That evening – that shocking change from David's joyful assurance to his last and mindless-seeming struggle – seems to me to demonstrate that word's full capacity. I think he did suffer in his dying. There was confusion, and there was sometimes pain; and after all these are a part of living, too. But he endured it, and in the end I think even permitted it, knowing that he'd got his leave.

~

In the preface to *The Book of the Craft of Dying*, there is a letter written by a young French soldier to his mother in 1917, shortly before he died at the front. He surveys death without hope, but all the same resolves to find illumination in whatever hours remain: 'The regiment next to ours has but forty men in it,' he writes. 'I dare not speak any more of hope. What one can demand is that one should have grace to exhaust all that the instant holds of good.'

Now: it is late on a Monday afternoon, and this instant holds some good. The days are getting dark and short; the winter-flowering almond can't be seen across the lawn but we leave the curtains open all the same. The red geraniums go on and on. My parents sit side by side against the wall; my mother knits, my father reads. Janey and Ruby drift from room to room, or lie companionably beyond the foot of the high white bed. All day we've been playing hymns for David, until Robert – who knows his father best – changes the music to rock 'n' roll. It's the hearing that goes last, he says, that's what they say.

We are attentive, with attention so devout it is like worship. David's breathing now follows a pattern which in due course we learn is so distinctive that it has a name:

it is Cheyne–Stokes respiration, which often signals approaching death. He exhales sighing breaths that look very like contentment, then for a time there is nothing and the blanket is unmoving on his chest. Robert, who'd been a police officer once, had often passed long nights watching the chests of sleeping prisoners rise and fall, prepared to rouse them and seek help if their breathing stopped; now, when the blanket goes still, we'll call no one. We lean towards David, breathless ourselves, thinking perhaps the moment has come – then he breathes again, and when I lean in I don't know what it is I'm hoping for. This watchfulness teaches me at last the kind of acquiescent patience which has always eluded me, and which T. S. Eliot writes of in *Four Quartets* – so I say to my soul: 'be still, and wait without hope'.

Then the death rattle begins. It's like nothing we ever heard before, but we know it when it comes because it could be no other thing: when David inhales, at those long and irregular intervals, it's as if there are magpies chattering in his throat. The volume is startling: who would have thought the old man to have so much noise in him? The cause of this is secretions of saliva which gather and thicken because he's got neither the strength nor the inclination to cough and clear it. When the carers come, they say not to be too troubled: the death rattle is more distressing for the family than the patient, and we can all be spared by an injection of Buscopan. Buscopan, we say, of all things! Frequently we laugh (it's the hearing that goes last: that's what they tell us). When

Robert and I go to fetch the prescription, we buy Eccles cakes because my father likes them and because we all deserve a treat. So we surround David, eating Eccles cakes and drinking coffee and speaking quietly: there's lamplight, music, the scent of sweet spices; the sound of my mother's knitting needles, of muted idle conversation and sighing dogs, and briefly my foolish mind interprets these signals as evidence of Christmas, and I am content. There's no world beyond the bungalow door, no life but this life, no hours but these hours. Death and its duties have become largely unremarkable; though now and then we're pierced with shock and sorrow. Once, my father – watching Robert moisten his father's mouth – turns suddenly away and is abruptly choked, and says privately to himself: 'I can't believe David is dying. I just can't believe it.'

It is one week since we saw the kindly consultant, and David laughed with me as he rested his tea on his stomach, and petted Janey at his side; he'll live through one more night.

The following day – a Tuesday, and the last of David's life – fine rain fell all morning and into the afternoon from low pale cloud made pearly sometimes by sunlight. The rain and the dim wet air beyond the windows enclosed us; it seemed more than ever we were sealed away from the world in a kind of hermitage. And it was on this morning, I recall, that David gripped my hand as I adjusted the covers and brought it to his mouth, and this mortified me, thinking perhaps he'd mistaken me for Jenny and was showing his affection after their long separation; so quite roughly I pulled my hand away, and it didn't occur to me until it was too late that in fact he might have thought I was holding a mug of water, and that he'd wanted something to drink. I think of this moment often, because it represents to me the absolute finality of death, which is the only final thing: I failed him then, and it is different from every other failure of mine because it's not possible to tell him I'm sorry, and there's no way to make it good.

That morning, too, the red-headed nurse sat for a time at the dining table, examined the papers which had accumulated there, and said: 'I think it's time now that we fitted David with a syringe driver.' This, he said, would deliver a continuous dose of the morphine, tranquillisers and Buscopan which were keeping David safe, as the consultant had said he would be. He'd be spared the repeated injections, which after all weren't easily done on a man so wasted, and we'd be relieved of our frequent and sometimes panicked visits to whichever pharmacies would serve us, and the brief periods of restlessness that troubled him. This required us to summon a doctor unfamiliar to us, and who came to the bungalow in a hurry to complete paperwork which authorised the use of the driver. However, some mistake was made with this paperwork which we never understood, but which prevented the red-headed nurse – diligent, authoritative, and openly exasperated by this small incompetence – from installing it. So Robert and I found ourselves late that afternoon in a GP's surgery without an appointment, bewildered by now with exhaustion and uncertain of the day or the hour, clutching a sheet of paper blotted with rain. The surgery was empty, and the lights in the waiting room were dim; the receptionist looked at us with astonishment. 'Yes?' she said – she was standing, she had somewhere to be.

'We phoned,' I said, in the beseeching way that came so easily to me in those days. 'My father-in-law is in palliative care, and we have a prescription for a syringe driver. But there's been a mistake, somebody needs to take a look.'

'Ah, right,' said the receptionist. Her face briefly illuminated: evidently she remembered the call, and that was a comfort. 'Yes,' she said; then gestured towards a man of perhaps my age, standing concealed between filing cabinets and placidly eating a banana. 'Yep?' he said. 'What is it?' He waved the banana.

'It's about a syringe driver,' I said; but then I was at a loss, because nobody had really been able to explain to us what the difficulty was – and meanwhile, for all I knew, David was swinging his brittle legs to the floor, and my mother was saying: 'It's all right, it's all right: somebody will be here soon.'

'You'd better come through,' the doctor said, shrugging, and then expertly tossing the peel of his banana into the bin with a gesture that appalled me because it was so careless and merry. And he was careless and merry, too, in his office, looking over the sheet of paper with an expression of cheerful bafflement: 'No idea what the trouble is here,' he said, 'no idea what they mean!' – then he seemed to identify a part of the form which could possibly account for the confusion, wrote something indecipherable in biro, then handed it back: 'There you go!' he said, smilingly. 'I expect that'll sort it. All right?'

'Thank you,' we said, because we ought to say it, and because we'd done what needed to be done – but in the car we looked at each other in astonishment, unable to grasp that a dying man's comfort could depend on this rather foolish stranger with his careless scribble, and his easy laugh.

Soon after this, we stood and watched as the district nurse, crouching beside the bed, lifted the floral quilt and the dog banket, and drew down David's pyjamas to reveal the greyish, wishbone curve of his thigh. The nurse inserted a needle ('All right, David; it's uncomfortable, I know') which was attached to a narrow tube terminating in a grey plastic box containing an immense syringe. This box contained a motor operated by a battery, which – almost silently, but never quite – would slowly depress the syringe, maintaining a constant supply of medication in David's blood. As the nurse carefully laid the plastic box of the driver flush against David's thigh, Robert lightly touched his father on the shoulder and said: 'Looks a bit like they're changing your print cartridge, Dad.' This made the nurse laugh, which permitted us all to laugh, too; and I imagine now that David, not quite crossed over to the other shore, heard his son's undiminished silliness, which was so like his own; and that if we'd only listened hard enough, we might have heard drifting up from the bed that absolutely particular laugh – *Heh! Heh!*

That day my parents went home. 'Goodbye, David,' they said, 'God bless you – God bless you'; my father prayed for him, and for Robert and me, then they each bent and kissed him with an easy and open affection. When I watched them go I both understood and envied the certainty of their faith. Those kisses were not final. They'd see him again, and in glory.

Then we were alone and companionable, we three. Robert and I were watchful, and it seemed to me that David was too, behind the glossy, deep-socketed lids of his eyes; now and then I saw some cognition pass fleetingly over that immobile face, and I wondered what he saw, and where he saw it. Soon we'd need to think about the funeral: we'd sing 'Great is Thy Faithfulness', of course, how could we not – and often David had said he would stipulate No Flowers, No Mourning. And we would choose a plain pine coffin: David had once said that a wicker eco-coffin was all very well, but really at the end of the day it was just a giant picnic hamper (we laughed; perhaps David laughed, too). A parcel had come, and when we opened it we found a small cross carved from olive wood, the upright and crosspiece blunted and smoothed as if by centuries of handling. There was no note, and though I later discovered it had been sent by a friend I'd known since I was a child, its nameless arrival felt like grace. I put it on David's chest, and left it there for a time; but this embarrassed me and would have embarrassed him, and soon I took it away, kept it in my pocket, and only returned it to David when he'd died.

Full dark on the outskirts of Norwich. Traffic sometimes beyond the bedroom window. Christmas lights faintly visible in bungalows elsewhere. We had run out of Wagon Wheels. The red geraniums needed water and were dropping their petals over the carpet, and in the empty heel of David's slippers. The moving mattress sighed; the syringe driver very faintly whirred. The figure on the bed, mythic and wonderful, seemed diminished by the hour, as if he were drifting over a horizon in the wall. Now and then the dogs rose, circled the bungalow in search of something, and settled again, never finding it. When Emmanuel came to us that night, his broad figure at the door and his weighty laptop already familiar, we made him tea, and watched him take up his post: 'He's quiet now,' we said, 'it's been a quiet day.' I went over to the high white bed. My watch was over. Little enough left of David now to lift the quilt and blanket. I stooped over him, and smoothed the downy hair which was tidier and more biddable now than it had ever been. Briefly I put my face beside his on the pillow; and 'It's all right, my darling,' I said. 'It's all right, Dad. We're going to be OK – if you have to go now, we're going to be all right.' I kissed his forehead. I cannot recall whether I cried. I went through to the other room and the mattress on the floor, and left Robert to say goodnight. (Let him have his father to himself.)

The novelist Iris Murdoch, in her work of moral philosophy *The Sovereignty of Good*, writes: 'Prayer is properly not petition, but simply an attention to God which is a form of love.' If, as I hope, she was right, it is true to say that this night was not like all the other nights, because it was the first night I prayed for David. It was not a petition. There were no words. It was only that my attention became fixed absolutely on David and on God, love equally divided between the two, who seemed to me then equally real – I lay on my back; I looked at the ceiling with its whirled white plaster, and thought it thin, gauzy, as if something might easily pass up through it. I found then that I was smiling, and that some curious stillness was settling in me which was like the stillness I feel when I am in water. I lifted my arms, without consciously lifting them – they rose regardless of my reason, or my faithlessness and disclination to prayer: it was as if I were holding David again, as I'd held him when he toppled from the bed or when agitation caused him to struggle – it was as if I were giving him to God. Then quickly the absurdity and hubris of this struck me, and I was ashamed. My arms dropped; I turned my back to the window, and fell very soon into profound sleep.

At three o'clock in the morning Emmanuel knocked on our bedroom door. This knocking was not quite frantic, but certainly it was urgent, and as telling as the tolling of a bell. We came to our feet without stumbling; we were already dressed. Robert opened the door. Emmanuel stood back to let us pass: 'David has died,' he said. 'He is dead.' We were all quiet for a time: so it has come, I thought. I had the sensation not that someone had departed, but that something had arrived.

We went quickly across the hall. One lamp was on; also there was bluish light from the open laptop screen. Robert went to the bed. I followed him. 'Dad?' said Robert – he put his hand on his father's shoulder. David was unchanged, because he had already changed. His mouth was open, his eyes were not; his forehead was high, smooth and gleaming. For a moment – and out of habit, not hope – we watched for the movement of his chest beneath the blanket. There was none. 'Oh Dad,' I said. Robert kissed him. So did I. His skin was warm. He hadn't been gone long. 'Goodbye, Dad,' we said. 'Oh, goodbye, goodbye.'

Emmanuel came forward. His white polo shirt was neatly tucked in. He stood beside us; he clasped his hands loosely in front of him. He looked with absolute and reverent attention at the figure in the bed. 'David?' His manner was grave: he had authority. 'We love you,' he said. 'Rest in everlasting peace.' He bowed; he turned away. He clasped Robert by the shoulder; he nodded at me. Then silently and quickly he packed up his laptop, took his coat down from the hook in the hall, and left us.

Now we were alone. We stood beside the bed – we moved away and returned to it over and over. How extraordinary it was, we said, to think he had gone. I held Robert, or he held me. There was relief, and there was loss – it was the saddest thing we'd ever seen, and the best thing we had ever done – all these things existing together undiminished, and never cancelling each other out. Now and then we touched David, and there was nothing to be seen that was frightening, there was no need to avert our eyes: it was only David, and Robert was not yet deprived of his father. I put the kettle on. How ordinary I was then! As I waited I phoned, for the final time, the community hub, and told them that David had died, and that I supposed somebody should come – only this time, I said, there was no rush. Sometimes cars passed and we wondered who was up at that hour, and why, and we loved them for their company. We exhausted all that the instant held of good. We opened the curtains: we looked west. Marvellous night, no moon – Orion passing over the bungalow, Mars burning behind the winter-flowering almond tree. And in the east behind us, soon enough: the late and inevitable morning.

PART THREE
Afterlife

I have here on my desk a disc of black glass which almost passes for obsidian. It is slightly convex, and measures five inches in diameter and a quarter of an inch deep; the rim is bound in brass, and there's a brass loop through which I could, if I wanted, pass a ribbon or a bit of string. It might be mistaken for a scrying mirror – the sort of thing the magician John Dee used in the court of Elizabeth to converse with angels. But no angels communicate with me: it's a Claude glass, and its only magic is a trick of the light.

The seventeenth-century artist Claude Lorrain, known to the English only as Claude, was once called by John Constable 'the most perfect landscape painter the world ever saw'. And though he kept his sketches in a book called the *Liber Veritatis* – that is, the *Book of Truth* – his paintings are not particularly truthful. The world according to Claude consists of ruins set always in the foreground, and never ruined enough to be spoiled; trees in full dark leaf surround them, and behind them mountains recede towards a lowering sun, or sometimes a port at high tide brings in white-sailed ships. Claude's light is forever fading, his trees forever windblown, his hills forever in shadow – everywhere there's a kind of radiant darkness, and colours that are muted and deep.

After his death, there was a brief fad for tourists to take with them on their travels a Claude glass – black, convex, backed in silver – which they could use to remake the world in the image of a Claude. They'd stand with their back to the view, examine the land contained in the circuit of the glass, and find the land more sombre, strange and lovely than fact.

In the weeks that followed David's death, Robert and I discovered that nothing was left unaltered by those nine days. Death became the Claude glass, curtailing and dimming the view: the world was at the same time darker, more perilous and more beautiful than we'd ever taken it to be – though in the unfinished fragments collected at the end of Christopher Hitchens's *Mortality*, there's a quotation from Saul Bellow suggesting that death's mirror clarifies, and does not obscure: 'Death is the dark backing that a mirror needs if we are able to see anything.' I'm still not certain whether those first few weeks, radiantly dark, gave a picture of life which was distorted, or finally true. Perhaps it was both.

David's funeral took place at an old Strict Baptist chapel down a narrow country lane, because his own church had no room for the coffin and the hearse. This chapel was soon to close for lack of a minister, and I suppose really it was an unremarkable place, its red bricks spalled and its small graveyard overgrown. But that day it seemed unbearably imposing and melancholy, the tipping gravestones casting shadows almost to the open door – I was sure I'd never heard a congregation sing with such sincerity and pathos, never before understood the absurd and terrible gravity of the top hats the undertakers wore, never loved my friends more sincerely than when I saw them distributed among the mourners they'd never met before, and never would again. When I stood to read Psalm 103 – 'Bless the Lord, Oh my soul: and all that is within me, bless his holy name' – the familiar phrases unmade and remade themselves as I read, and left me dismantled, so that I was unable to go on: 'As for man, his days are as grass: as a flower of the field, so he flourisheth. For the wind passeth over it, and it is gone; and the place thereof shall know it no more.' The sight of David's coffin, with his name in full inscribed on a brass plate, was as shocking to me as if I'd never before known there was such a thing as a coffin. 'It contains him,' I thought, sitting very close nearby, 'that actually contains David, he is in there' – it was monstrous, I thought, I could never have imagined such a thing. The coffin had contained David, and David had contained time – years in the dim flat with its lines of washing in the yard, years coming home to Jenny on the Fenchurch Street line, years in Yarmouth sitting at the rim of the sea and never any further – and now the container was sealed, and the time could never be recovered. Soon I began to think of myself as a container for time, never knowing my capacity or how much there was left to fill: I saw the hours and minutes vanish, and wondered what value they had. Again and again I returned to the resolve of Tagore's speaker in *Gitanjali*:

> *On the day when death will knock at thy door what wilt thou offer him?*

Oh, I will set before my guest the full vessel of my life —
I will never let him go with empty hands.

Often in the following months I'd be seized with terror that I was seeing some person or object for the last time, because the fact of my mortality became the first principle from which everything followed. One afternoon the pigeons that populate Norwich's market square struck me as miraculous: if I'm dying, I thought, which I may well be, I'll never see a pigeon again — so I looked for a long time with a kind of grieving wonder at their necks bruised with an oil-on-water shine, their scarred feet bright as branched coral, their spread wings dissolving into mercury. The future became foreshortened, as if all my life I'd been walking down a corridor with lights overhead diminishing in the far distance to a point, and these had suddenly gone out, save for the two or three overhead. 'We'll go next year,' friends would say, or 'One day I'd like to do this thing, or that thing,' and I'd look at them in bewilderment, because there was no next year, no one day: there was only the fragile and continuous now.

In his poem *'De Corporis Resurrectione'* — that is, 'On the Resurrection of the Body' — the poet John Burnside (who died before he reached seventy) inhabits a world in which the dead survive their dying by transformations into moments of fleeting and everyday grace:

> *. . . the gradual dead*
> *drifting between the trees like gusts of wind*
> *and finding a visible form*

> *an approximate colour:*
> *aconite; meltwater; cinnabar; Prussian blue;*
> *the dead we have named and buried*
> *breaking like waves*
> *on sandstone and leaf*
> *on tree-bark and rusted iron.*

I would like to say I found David in the sunlight that sometimes dissolves the wall, or the speedwell that was early the following spring, dispersed over the lawns as if it had come down with the rain, but I never did. He had died, and he was absent: annihilated absolutely, or gone from us – as he believed – to his long home in glory.

Soon the Claude glass broke, and the disbelieving, dreamlike effects of those first weeks was replaced with sometimes unwelcome clarity – now there seemed to be an audible ticking everywhere, visible signs of decay, mortal danger in the turn of a stair, the whole world marked with a yellow label showing its expiry date. It isn't that I'd previously thought we were immortal. 'Death is the greatest fact in life,' writes Frances Comper. 'It faces us from our earliest consciousness. There is nothing startling in it to the child's mind.'

So we'd always known we were mortal – but to know something is not necessarily to understand it. We know for example that every action is met with an equal and opposite reaction, because Newton tells us so – but if with every step we fully understood that the earth, moving as it is through space, was pressing upward on the soles of our feet, we'd never get far beyond the door. And if every day on waking we fully understood that there's a limit set on our time, which might be either in decades or in minutes, I think we'd go mad first with wonder, then with grief: never again that unwelcome morning alarm, never again this black coffee in this chipped cup, never again those bin lorries coming down the street. We knew David would die, as we'll all die, but we had never grasped it, and because of this, as we were out walking the dogs one night, I stopped abruptly in the road and said aloud, 'David is dead? He has died, he really has'; because despite having sat for hours with his body at sunrise it was necessary to state it again and again before we could comprehend it.

In the months and years that followed, I saw Robert – an orphan now, without sisters or brothers or children – move between disbelief that he'd lost his father, and sudden pained comprehension. Once, standing in our kitchen as I cooked, he told me he felt he'd begun to cease to exist, as if he were fading out of a photograph. And one morning as I came to the end of writing this book, after our whippet Janey was put to sleep as she lay curled in my lap turning her fogged and trusting eyes from my face to his, Robert drove out to the bungalow where David had lived and died, and then – without really meaning to do it – he went on to the Morrisons where David had shopped, and brought home the plastic bags for which he'd always found another use.

I wonder as I write (the Claude glass is smeared with my thumbprint; Jenny and David watch me from the confines of their silver frame) what authority I have to speak about death. It isn't wisdom I have, it's only experience; and experience of only one death. It doesn't escape me that David was not young – that he was not extinguished in an instant on a motorway, or in some freakish incident at home. I've known of other deaths, which even the most acquiescent believer or stoic rationalist might think unnatural and unjust: the brilliant and loving young playwright who died, still writing, of a brain tumour; the husband who heard a noise and found his wife dead at the foot of the stairs; the man who died protractedly of pancreatic cancer and left five sons behind. There are kinds of death which are violent, graceless, and swift, that can never be prepared for. I remember for example a story in my family that two young brothers enlisted when the Great War began, the elder lying about the younger's age so they could go together to the front, then coming home without him – one loss in the incomprehensible scale of losses to war in those years, and in all the years since.

So I am still standing by the gate, and I keep it open, because there are things I want to tell you. I want to tell you that even a good and easeful death may have its indignities and pains, but to know this – to have seen it – is to fear death less, not more. I am not like the Ancient Mariner, casting the shadow of his albatross over the wedding guests; I'm trying to shed light. David I think had as good an end as can ever be hoped for, with his body and his spirits comforted, but all the same: he struggled. Now when I hear of 'dignity in dying' as I often do, the phrase troubles me with its imprecision, which comes close to dishonesty – it is as if it were possible to promise a woman dignity in birth. Even a child will overhear talk of morning sickness and labour pains, so that they become familiar; and if these things are feared and mitigated against as far as possible, they are not mysterious. The baby, also, struggles to be born – it is a shock for an infant to arrive unasked into life, to take the first breath, to learn how to seek after food. Then life follows, and has its pains and indignities – illnesses which are painful but not mortal, broken bones, disappointments, falls from grace: all the ordinary sorrow that comes with being here at all. Since it is a struggle to be born, and since no life can be lived without struggle, is it reasonable to imagine it is possible to die without a struggle, however brief? If you live, it is as necessary to die as it was to be born – so dying is a part of living, and like living it has its events, both difficult and marvellous. This ought not to be frightening, but comforting in its way: the craft of dying requires skills learned by living, and learning how to live may teach you how to die.

Still: I don't think it probable that familiarity with dying can remove the fear of death. Does our familiarity with living remove our fear of experiencing pain, or loss, or disappointment? What I mean is that it may be possible to bring the act of dying into the scope of living, and so fear its events and its struggles no more than life's other events. Delphine Horvilleur in her reflections on dying warns against the simple models supposed to take a patient neatly from the stage of denial to the stage of resignation:

> Each individual's trajectory in confronting death is unique. There can be no possible standardization to sum up the gamut of human emotions, no uniform model for each and every human trajectory as death looms.

If we are too various and surprising to create a kind of standard model of dying, there is all the same a kind of fellowship among those who've intimately witnessed death. In the years since David died, as I've told stories and sought them out, I've been consoled by what is held in common. There is the refusal of food, or of all food except one bewilderingly longed-for thing – then the still more bewildering refusal of water, and all of this lasting for days; there is the curious sense of withdrawal into a private world – then the death rattle, the planes of the skull appearing as if overnight, the improbable quantities of urine; the turns into sweetness or uncomprehending strength or both; the desiccating lips and hands. Often there are moments of release and offering-up, like my wordless prayer from the mattress on the floor among the boxes of stamps – often loved ones will give the dying permission to die, and find death follows within hours. Then, too, there is the fellowship of the undertakers, with their sombre plain-clothes ambulances and their kind and practical rituals: the body taken out always feet first; the bedding always removed from the deathbed, and set neatly aside in a pile, to spare the bereaved the sight of fluids demarcating the body's absence. A widow once took me by the shoulders and said, 'Why did nobody tell us? Why did nobody say?' – look at us, we said to each other: we are women, we ought to have seen it all before.

―⁓―

Some weeks ago the dogs woke me in the small hours because our cat Mrs Hudson had brought in a rat. It was perhaps a third of her size, and it wriggled and shrieked in her jaws. For days I'd slept badly, and was appalled by the noise and the struggle, and having shooed her out with her prey, I slammed the bedroom door; but I lay awake listening in horror as the tormented rat screamed in the room next door, where David's stamp collection was piled high in the white plastic boxes which were the last remaining evidence of his presence in the house. Eventually the screaming stopped, and I drifted into a sleep which was uneasy because it was guilty. The following morning I searched half-heartedly for the rat, but it was hopeless: boxes and papers were stacked from door to window, and besides Mrs Hudson was by now subdued, and nursing a scratch on her nose – probably it had freed itself, and was adventuring in the garden where the plants were dying back. But after a day or so, a dreadful smell began to come from that room. Robert knew it well, from those years in the police: 'Oh that's death,' he said placidly, 'there's nothing like it.' And there was nothing like it, nothing at all – a curious gaseous smell like spilled petrol, but with something sweetish in there, and base notes of rotting vegetable matter. It drifted out of the study as if it had substance, and was visible; after a day of this I began to be obsessed with the nature of an odour, and wanted to know what matter a smell consists of, if any (it occurred to me then there was a time I might have phoned David, and he could have told me). 'It's molecules,' I said to Robert, 'we are taking in molecules from the rat' – it had died, but was not dead: it was distributing itself, setting electrical impulses firing in the receptors in my nose, affecting the matter of my body and altering my frame of mind no less than if it had run across my bare foot. I thought then of the Buddhist model of life and death – of life constituting a wave which for a moment exists as a solitary thing before collapsing back to be distributed in the wide sea: the rat had taken one form, and was now taking another, and this form was now part of me.

On the third day – when we could no longer tell whether the smell remained in the air, or whether we were in some way stained by it – Robert called me upstairs, because he'd found the rat in a large blue box containing papers and photographs that were all to do with David. Together we looked in like mourners flanking an open grave. The rat seemed not to have rotted at all: its body was plump, its fawn pelt glossy, its naked tail and curled paws an identical pale pink. 'It's beautiful,' I said. 'Poor thing: it's lovely, and fought so hard to live.' It had died on its back on the order of service for David's funeral, and its exquisite, clever paws curled towards the photograph in which David's shy, dimpled smile was unstained. Since there is nothing can happen to me which is not immediately sorted and categorised into material, I began to laugh: 'The trouble is,' I said, 'nobody is going to believe this, are they?'

Now, when I pass the door to that room, I think how beautiful the rat was, and how it had begged for its life – of how it had been born blind, and then learned to distinguish one thing from another, and taken pleasure in its food and sleep; of the terror it had endured, and the exhausted consolation of the dark place where it had died. Then it occurs to me that for one hundred and twenty years families have lived in that house and passed through that room, and often I wonder what other lives ended there, and will end there; whether perhaps I will die there too, though I'd prefer my last bed to be made up in the room downstairs where I write, and keep a piano I never play – put the bed within reach of my desk, I'll say: have me facing the Japanese maple in the garden that my mother gave me.

These days I carry these thoughts with me and am astonished to find I'm no sadder now than I was before I had them, only that I've been moved by David's death – picked up, and put down in another place. I am a container for time, filling swiftly and with no idea of my limit. My faith wanes and waxes: I am no wiser than I ever was, it is only that I've seen more than I'd ever seen. Sometimes I stand at an upstairs window after dark when the city is getting ready for bed, and watch the lights go out one by one in rooms where strangers live. And if I stand there long enough I find, in compensation for the gathering dark, other lights arriving out of nothing – the passage of a car turning for home, lamps switched on in bathrooms and bedrooms on the outskirts of town, streetlights marking roads I know quite well. Then I imagine I've walked out of the city and up what passes in Norfolk for a hill, and that I can see spread all around me this same pattern going on over and over: lights, everywhere, coming on where there was no light, then shining for a moment or an hour before fading slowly to an ember, or being suddenly extinguished. On and on it goes, far ahead and behind me, over borders, horizons, seas, summoned up and going out in their own time – illuminating barely an inch or fully half a mile, and each light particular, never to be repeated or replaced: all those other lights. All those other towns.

Acknowledgements

Thank you to Robert Perry, my husband and my friend, for his patience and courage.

Thank you – with all my heart, and until the day I also get my leave – to Sam Guglani, Luther Chaplin, David Butler, Maureen Butler, Ruth Butler, David Harry Lane, Sally Roe, Jude Johncock, Ben Johncock, Chris Gribble, Sarah Hall, and Michelle Woolfenden; to my sisters; and to all our friends who were present in all kinds of ways.

Thank you to David's family on earth, and in Christ.

Thank you to Esther Laver, for the Latin.

Thank you to Louisa Yates, for the courage.

Thank you to the Norfolk Hospice and to the NHS, and to every practitioner who came to David in those days with their competence and kindness. Thank you, Emmanuel.

Thank you to Jenny Hewson, Hannah Westland, Susan Golomb and Caroline Zancan for meeting David in this book with affection and sorrow and laughter. Thank you to Sarah-Jane Forder, Suzanne Dean, Graeme Hall and all at Jonathan Cape and Mariner for everything they have done to bring this book to its readers.

Thank you, David. Thank you, Jenny. We loved you.

About the Author

Sarah Perry is the internationally bestselling author of the novels *Enlightenment, Melmoth, The Essex Serpent* and *After Me Comes the Flood*, and the essay *Essex Girls*. She is a winner of the Waterstones Book of the Year Award and the British Book of the Year Award. *Enlightenment* was longlisted for the Booker Prize 2024 and her other work has been nominated for major literary prizes including the Women's Prize for Fiction, the Dylan Thomas Prize, the Folio Prize and the Costa Novel Award. She is a Fellow of the Royal Society of Literature. *Death of an Ordinary Man* is her first full-length work of non-fiction.